COLORADO
LAKE
HIKES
SECOND EDITION

Upper Chicago Lake.

THE COLORADO
MOUNTAIN CLUB
GUIDEBOOK

COLORADO LAKE HIKES

SECOND EDITION

DAVE MULLER

The Colorado Mountain Club Press
Golden, Colorado

Colorado Lake Hikes
© 2008 Dave Muller

PUBLISHED BY:

The Colorado Mountain Club Press
710 Tenth Street, #200
Golden, Colorado 80401
303-279-3080 ext. 2
email: cmcpress@cmc.org

Founded in 1912, The Colorado Mountain Club is the largest outdoor recreation, education, and conservation organization in the Rocky Mountains. Look for our books at your local bookstore or outdoor retailer or online at www.cmc.org

Alan Bernhard—design and composition
Claire Bow—photo editor
John Gascoyne—copyeditor & proofreader
Alan Stark—publisher

CONTACTING THE PUBLISHER
We would appreciate it if readers would alert us to any errors or outdated information by contacting us at the address above.

DISTRIBUTED TO THE BOOK TRADE BY:

Mountaineers Books
1001 SW Klickitat Way, Suite 201, Seattle, WA 98134, 800-553-4453, www.mountaineersbooks.org

TOPOGRAPHIC MAPS are copyright 2008 and were created using National Geographic TOPO! Outdoor Recreation software. 800-962-1643, www.natgeomaps.com

COVER IMAGE: Finch Lake. Photo by Alan Stark.

We gratefully acknowledge the financial support of the people of Colorado through the Scientific and Cultural Facilities District of greater metropolitan Denver for our publishing activities.

ISBN: 978-0-9799663-1-6

Printed in Canada

WARNING: Although there has been an effort to make trail descriptions in this book as accurate as possible, some discrepancies may exist between the text and the trails in the field. Hiking in mountainous areas is a high-risk activity. This guidebook is not a substitute for your experience and common sense. The users of this guidebook assume full responsibility for their own safety. Weather, terrain conditions, and individual abilities must be considered before undertaking any of the hikes in this guide.

CONTENTS

FRONT RANGE

ESTES PARK AREA

IDAHO SPRINGS / GEORGETOWN AREA

WINTER PARK / FRASER AREA

GRANBY / GRAND LAKE AREA

STEAMBOAT SPRINGS / WALDEN / YAMPA AREA

SILVERTHORNE / DILLON / ALMA AREA

BUENA VISTA / SALIDA AREA

LEADVILLE AREA

VAIL / EAGLE AREA

ACKNOWLEDGMENTS

Thanks to my many hiking companions whose encouragement and good conversation on the trail made this book possible. Alan Stark and The Colorado Mountain Club improved the first edition of this book and have my gratitude. Jackie, my loving spouse, and my children often accompanied me on these hikes. Most of all I thank the source, the Creator of the Universe, who provided the wonderful Colorado playground and the equipment to enjoy it.

PREFACE

The Colorado mountains have been a major part of my life for the past thirty-nine years. Earlier family hikes progressed to more strenuous outings and led to two books—*Colorado Mountain Hikes for Everyone, Colorado Mountain Ski Tours and Hikes*—and a weekly hiking or crosscountry skiing column in *The Denver Post* from 1988 until 2005.

My purpose in these writings has been to provide specific information and good directions to the hike, and to enable more people to enjoy this wonderful and accessible playground we have in Colorado. Wild natural beauty can promote growth in personal consciousness, health, and well being, as well as reverence for the earth.

As I have grown older, my hiking to summits has evolved toward greater interest in Colorado's many beautiful lakes. By devoting this entire book to lake hikes, my wish is to give them the greater attention that they deserve and to provide counterbalance to the emphasis on Colorado's peaks, especially the Fourteeners.

INTRODUCTION

Colorado is noted for its high peaks. Visitors from all over the world come to climb its summits and ski its slopes.

The beautiful lakes lying beneath these mountains are often overlooked. Collecting the streams and snowmelt from above, the lakes provide homes for fish and refuge for birds and other wildlife. Lakes of various sizes and shapes can be found in rocky bowls, high basins, or open valleys. Some are man-made to prevent floods, store water, and provide recreation.

This book describes one hundred hikes to 148 different bodies of water. All have been visited on foot by the author.

By experiencing these Colorado treasures, the hiker hopefully will find renewal of spirit and a greater connection to our majestic mountain environment and its source.

A hike to a mountain lake provides a different ambience than a mountain ascent. The lake hiker is generally more relaxed, and often more aware of the surroundings. Lake hikes are usually less demanding and rarely require technical equipment or special caution. The exhilaration of the summit contrasts with the serenity of the mountain lake.

All the lakes in this book have trails leading close to their shores, are located on public land, and are open to everyone. Occasionally, a fee is charged at the trailhead by a governmental agency. The hikes are grouped by a nearby town or village, although some are closer than others, starting with the Front Range.

HIKE SPECIFICATIONS

The difficulty of a hike depends mainly on its length and elevation gain. The highest elevation is also important. Often the high point of a lake hike will be higher than the lake itself. Visitors from a lower elevation should realize that it takes several weeks to acclimate fully to higher altitudes. Therefore, hike to the lower elevations and the easier destinations initially, and then gradually increase both elevation and length. The hiking times stated are those of the author when he hiked to each lake and do not include breaks which are longer than those needed to catch one's breath. Hiking times are offered as a reference point and not a standard. Remember that fatigue will usually increase the return times.

The elevation gain includes the extra feet at segments of the trail where elevation is lost on the ascent and gained on the descent.

Four levels of difficulty are listed: easy, moderate, more difficult, and most difficult. Adverse weather and trail conditions will increase difficulty.

Various maps can be used for each hike. The 7.5 minute USGS map is the most detailed, but the Trails Illustrated map is often more current, damage-resistant, and useful. The county maps offer more contour detail than the National Forest maps, but are less current. The map of a specific national, state, or county park, if available, is often the most helpful.

TRAILS

All hikes in this book have good trails. If you lose a trail, back up and try to find where you lost the way. Following a creek to or from its lake source can be a backup plan. Hiking off trail is called bushwhacking and requires a compass. Outdoor people owe a great debt to the trail makers and map makers whose labor enables us to enter these playgrounds so deeply.

ROCKY MOUNTAIN NATIONAL PARK

Many of these hikes lie within Rocky Mountain National Park. The trails in the park are generally well marked and maintained, and the scenery is usually extraordinary. Detailed information can be obtained at the park visitor centers. Pets and vehicles are forbidden on the park trails. The grandeur of Rocky Mountain National Park draws great numbers of visitors, especially in the summer. Pay the entrance fee, avoid weekends and holidays, if possible, and brave the crowds. It's worth it.

HIKING SEASON

Generally, one can hike to some of these lakes from April until November. Snowshoes can lengthen the season. Lower elevations are recommended in the early and late seasons. You must usually wait until late June or early July to reach some of the higher lakes.

RECOMMENDED EQUIPMENT

Good footwear with adequate tread and ankle support, head covering, adequate water (at least 1.5 quarts per person per half day), a compass, sunscreen, a backpack and adequate food and protection from the cold and wet are strongly advised. A flashlight, map, matches, whistle, survival blanket, and reflector add little weight and may be lifesaving in an emergency. Cell phones have often helped to avert tragedy when a hiker becomes lost or injured.

CAUTION

No guidebook can replace the good judgment and responsibility of the hiker. Be sure of what you are doing and where you are going. Forest rangers can advise you. Dangerous weather can quickly envelop you and lead to confusion and bad decision-making. It is very easy to get lost, and even a short fall can be catastrophic. Be careful, be aware and enjoy!

PUBLISHER'S NOTE

First, many thanks to Claire Bow for coordinating the efforts of more than thirty volunteer photographers from the Colorado Mountain Club. Second, thanks to the following photographers:

Joe Aldridge	John Lacher	Doug Reese
Frank Burzynski	Joe Leahy	Mathew Rick
Dave Callais	Ryan Lewandowski	Rosalyn Sample
Dave Cooper	Ulli Limpitlaw	Rick Schroeder
Jay Fell	Darren Lingle	Glenn Silva
Tim Gattone	Mike Matson	Maria Smith
Ginni Greer	Cathy McKeen	Bill Stone
Judy Herzanek	Jeff Miller	David Thomas
David Hite	Kathy Pillmore	Keifer Thomas
Bernard Hohman	Sandra Portner	Bob Watkins
Alex Hudgins	Penelope Purdy	Rich Webb
Keith Jensen	Clif Reed	Cameron Wenzel

Special thanks to the people at National Geographic Maps for the use of their TOPO! Outdoor Recreation Software for both mock-ups and final maps.

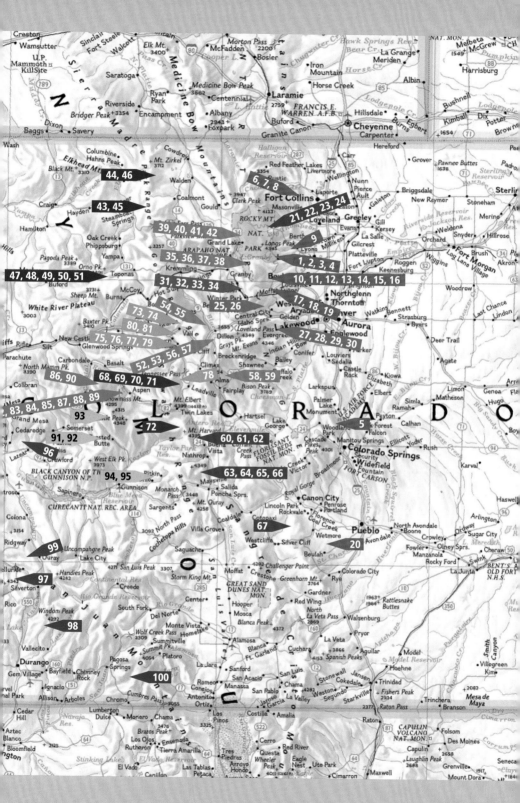

15

1. Finch Lake

ROUND-TRIP DISTANCE	8 miles
HIKING TIME	Out in 110 minutes, back in 94 minutes
STARTING ELEVATION	8,940 feet
HIGHEST ELEVATION	10,165 feet
ELEVATION GAIN	1975 feet (includes 750 extra feet)
DIFFICULTY	Moderate
MAPS	Trails Illustrated, Rocky Mountain National Park, Number 200 Allens Park 7.5 minute Boulder County

COMMENT: This lovely hike in the southeastern corner of Rocky Mountain National Park is the shortest of several routes to Finch Lake. An added bonus is the lack of a park fee requirement at this newer trailhead. The trail is well defined and signs telling directions and distances occur at key intersections. On the way to the lake, you pass through 0.25 mile of burnt forest from a September 1978 fire. As in all of Rocky Mountain National Park, pets, guns, and bicycles are forbidden on the trail.

GETTING THERE: Drive to Allenspark, northwest of Lyons and south of Estes Park, on Colorado 7. Turn west into Allenspark near the crest of a hill and set your mileage to zero. (This turnoff onto Colorado 7 is 18.4 miles from the Colorado 7 and U.S. 36 intersection in Lyons.) Within 75 yards of your turn, keep right and then quickly turn right again on County Road 90, which becomes the South Skinner Road. Follow this main, well-graded road to mile 1.3 and then turn right on the Meadow Mountain Road. After another 0.1 mile on this road, turn right into the Allenspark Trail area and park.

THE HIKE: From the parking area, pass by a signboard and follow the trail to the west. Ascend through the forest and keep left at a fork 0.8 mile from the trailhead and, later, take the trail on the left at a four-way intersection at mile 1.8. Continue south and soon enter the 0.25 mile of burnt, bare forest. Chiefs Head Peak, Pagoda Mountain, Longs Peak, and Mount Meeker can be seen across the valley on the right. After reaching a high point, follow the trail as it descends to lovely Finch Lake. Some named peaks can be seen from here: Copeland Mountain to the west-southwest, Elk Tooth and

Ogalalla Peak and Mount Copeland from the east side of Finch Lake.   PHOTO BY ALAN STARK

Ogalalla Peak to the southwest, and Saint Vrain Mountain to the south-southeast. Unless you wish to continue on the trail to Pear Lake, return as you came.

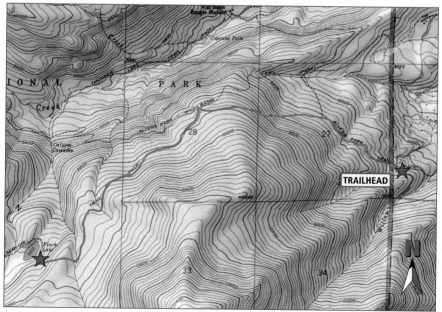

Finch Lake.

2. Chasm Lake

ROUND-TRIP DISTANCE	8.4 miles
HIKING TIME	Up in 110 minutes, down in 90 minutes
STARTING ELEVATION	9,400 feet
HIGHEST ELEVATION	11,850 feet
ELEVATION GAIN	2,706 feet (includes 256 extra feet)
DIFFICULTY	Moderate
MAPS	Trails Illustrated, Rocky Mountain National Park, Number 200 or Longs Peak, Number 301 Longs Peak 7.5 minute Larimer County Number 3 Boulder County

COMMENT: Hiking to Chasm Lake offers many rewards. The trail is excellent and very scenic. Before the final trail fork, you are likely to encounter hikers trying to summit nearby Longs Peak, Colorado's northernmost Fourteener. And, at Chasm Lake, the view of the massive east face of Longs Peak, called "The Diamond," is awe inspiring. Chasm Lake drains into Peacock Pool, the Roaring Fork of Tahosa Creek, and the Ralph Price Reservoir.

GETTING THERE: Drive on Colorado 7, either 24.2 miles from the west end of Lyons, or 9.6 miles south from the junction of Colorado 7 with U.S. 36 in Estes Park. Then turn west for 1.1 miles on the good road and park at the Longs Peak Ranger Station, which is often full of cars.

THE HIKE: Begin south on the excellent trail from the ranger station. Pass a trail register before the trail turns northwest. After a steep 0.5 mile, take the left fork at a sign. (The right fork leads to the Eugenia Mine and the Estes Cone.) Continue up through the forest and in 1.3 more miles cross a bridge at a small waterfall. After 0.7 miles more you will pass timberline and reach another fork and sign. Ascend left, as the right fork goes to Battle Mountain Campground. After another mile through Mills Moraine, you arrive at a third signed fork. Go left and lose some elevation as you follow a shelf trail below impressive, steep rocky cliffs. (The right fork leads to Longs Peak in 4 miles.) Cross over Columbine Falls and follow the trail past the Chasm Lake Patrol Station. The trail then follows cairns steeply up over rocks to the west before becoming faint and passing to the right of a huge boulder. Chasm Lake then lies to your right. The east face of Longs Peak is awesome above

Chasm Lake and the Longs Peak "Diamond" above.

PHOTO BY BOB WATKINS

and to the southwest. Mount Lady Washington hovers above to the northwest and Mount Meeker to the south. Retrace your route back to the trailhead.

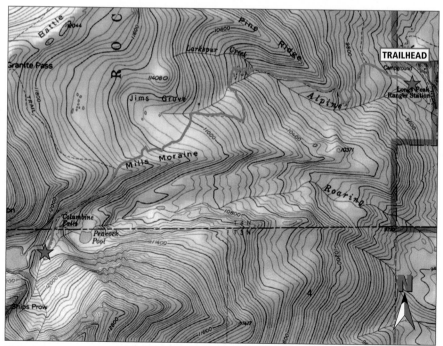

Chasm Lake.

3. Ouzel Lake and Bluebird Lake

ROUND-TRIP DISTANCE	4.9 miles to Ouzel Lake, 1.7 miles further to Bluebird Lake (Total up 6.6 miles) Back to Trailhead in 6.3 miles
HIKING TIME	Up to Ouzel Lake in 112 minutes, then to Bluebird Lake in 55 minutes (Total up in 167 minutes) Down in 132 minutes
STARTING ELEVATION	8,500 feet
HIGHEST ELEVATION	11,000 feet
ELEVATION GAIN	3,620 feet (includes 1,120 extra feet)
DIFFICULTY	More difficult
MAPS	Trails Illustrated, Rocky Mountain National Park, Number 200 Allens Park 7.5 minute Isolation Peak 7.5 minute Boulder County

COMMENT: Here are two lakes in wonderful Rocky Mountain National Park that are named for birds. The route takes you by much beautiful, flowing water to two lovely lakes below impressive rocky peaks. Weapons, pets and bicycles are forbidden on park trails.

GETTING THERE: From the west side of Lyons at the intersection of U.S. 36 and Colorado 7, drive west and north on Colorado 7 for 20.6 miles and turn left at the sign to the Wild Basin Ranger Station. After 0.4 mile on this paved road, turn right onto a good dirt road, pay an entry fee and follow the road for 2.2 more miles to its end and parking at the Wild Basin Ranger Station and the trailhead. Regular cars can easily reach this parking area.

THE HIKE: Start on foot to the south-southwest and follow the excellent trail past short side trails on the left, to Lower and Upper Copeland Falls. With Ouzel Creek on your left, cross a bridge to the other side, at 1.3 miles from the trailhead. Ascend another 0.5 mile to the Calypso Cascades, a scenic area of flowing water, and a sign about extensive forest fire of August 1978. Keep right and cross two bridges. The trail then passes through the burn area from the 1978 fire. After 0.9 mile, beyond the Calypso Cascades, cross a bridge below dramatic Ouzel Falls and proceed another 0.4 mile to a signed fork. You continue up to the left (west), as the right fork leads up the valley toward Thunder Lake and the Lion Lakes. The trail then ascends to an open burned area with great vistas of the surrounding peaks. After 1.3 miles from the last fork, you reach another signed fork. Descend left (north) 0.5 mile to

Bluebird Lake.

PHOTO BY TIM GATTONE

Ouzel Lake at the foot of Mount Copeland to the south. Enjoy the beauty and then proceed north 0.25 mile, without a trail, to regain the trail. Then turn left and continue up the valley. The last 1.5 miles to Bluebird Lake is especially scenic as the trail gets rockier and steeper. Cairns often mark the trail. At Bluebird Lake there is a sign explaining how the dam was removed for environmental reasons in 1989. Isolation Peak is prominent past the lake to the southwest. Tahana Peak towers above northwest. Return by your lengthy but very interesting ascent route, bypassing Ouzel Lake.

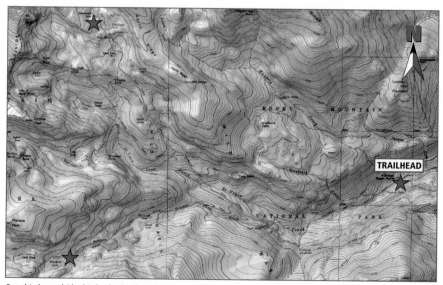

Ouzel Lake and Bluebird Lake (trail on the lower left),
Lion Lake One and Two and Snowbank Lake (upper trail on left).

4. Lion Lake Number One, Lion Lake Number Two, and Snowbank Lake

ROUND-TRIP DISTANCE	7.0 miles to Lion Lake Number One, 0.5 mile more to Lion Lake Number Two, and 0.3 mile more to Snowbank Lake (Total 7.8 miles)
HIKING TIME	Up in 237 minutes, down in 146 minutes
STARTING ELEVATION	8,500 feet
HIGHEST ELEVATION	11,521 feet
ELEVATION GAIN	3,671 feet (includes 650 extra feet)
DIFFICULTY	Most difficult
MAPS	Trails Illustrated, Rocky Mountain National Park, Number 200 Allens Park 7.5 minute Isolation Peak 7.5 minute Boulder County

COMMENT: If you enjoy rushing water alongside your hiking trail, the Wild Basin Area of Rocky Mountain National Park is for you. For a shorter hike, the walk as far as Calypso Cascades and Ouzel Falls is ideal. The long hike, which goes all the way to Snowbank Lake, gives you even more roaring streams. Snow lingers in the upper reaches of this trek well into July. Therefore, wait until the second half of August or September to experience this beautiful hike. The trails of Rocky Mountain National Park are well marked by signs, which give directions and often distances. Pets, bicycles, and weapons are forbidden on trails within the national park.

GETTING THERE: From the west end of Lyons, leave U.S. 36 and take the left fork on Colorado 7. Follow this road up past Allenspark for 20.6 miles and turn left into the Wild Basin Area. After 0.4 mile from Colorado 7, turn right, pay an entry fee, and follow the good dirt road 2.2 more miles up the valley and park at road end near the trailhead.

THE HIKE: Your trek begins to the south from a signboard. Cross Hunters Creek and proceed up the valley with North Saint Vrain Creek on your left. Cross a bridge and delight in the racing water, just before arriving at the scenic Calypso Cascades at mile 1.8. Take the trail to the right and pass through a burnt area from the large fire of September 1978, and reach Ouzel Falls at mile 2.7. Continue on this lovely trail another 0.4 mile to a signed

Lion Lake Number Two.

PHOTO BY MIKE MATSON

fork. The trail on the left leads to Ouzel Lake and Bluebird Lake. Continue straight to another crossing of North Saint Vrain Creek and several campsites, just beyond at mile 3.5. It will now be 1.3 more gradual miles through thick forest before you reach a key junction at mile 4.8. At the sign, take the right (northwest) fork and ascend steeply toward Lion Lake Number One. (The left fork leads to Thunder Lake.) The trail rises and curves for 2.2 miles before passing a small pond on the left and reaching gorgeous Lion Lake Number One from above. Mount Alice is the striking pyramidal summit to the west-northwest. Continue by trail along the right side of the lake and then cross a creek on the left. Cairns mark the way up to gushing Trio Falls, where you cross the outflow to the left and then ascend to a rocky cut on the right. Follow the cairns to the left side of lovely Lion Lake Number Two. Continue along the left side of the lake toward the creek, which feeds the lake, and pick your way easily up to the left of this creek to Snowbank Lake. There is no trail for this final segment, but an occasional cairn may be seen. The snow bank at the far end of the lake gives it its name. Chiefs Head Peak provides the rocky wall to the north. The long return will be by the ascent route.

SEE MAP PAGE 21

5. Stanley Canyon Reservoir

ROUND-TRIP DISTANCE	4.2 miles
HIKING TIME	Up in 71 minutes, down in 47 minutes
STARTING ELEVATION	7,480 feet
HIGHEST ELEVATION	8,860 feet
ELEVATION GAIN	1,580 feet (includes 100 extra feet each way)
DIFFICULTY	More difficult
MAPS	Trails Illustrated, Pikes Peak/Cañon City, Number 137 Cascade 7.5 minute El Paso County Number 1 Pike National Forest

COMMENT: The Air Force Academy allows easy access to the Stanley Canyon Trailhead. The hike up the canyon is steep and passes amid beautiful rock formations to terminate at the Stanley Canyon Reservoir, which is also known as Reservoir Number Two. Connecting trails lead to other nearby reservoirs.

GETTING THERE: From Interstate 25 north of Colorado Springs, take exit 150 and follow the southern access road into the U.S. Air Force Academy. After 2.7 miles from I-25 on this main road, go left onto Pine Drive. Follow Pine Drive for 4.0 miles and go left onto an unmarked, good dirt road on the left, opposite the Academy Hospital. Keep straight on this dirt road at 0.4 mile and park at the trailhead 0.8 mile from Pine Drive.

THE HIKE: From the parking area, begin your hike to the southwest on Trail 707. Follow the road as it quickly curves to the right and ascends over rough terrain. Within 125 yards, leave this road and take a trail on the left that enters the forest and rises steeply into the canyon to the west. Within 0.5 mile, keep left at a fork with the creek below on your left side. After about 1 mile, pass to the left of some impressive rock formations. Make two creek crossings and reach an open valley at 1.5 miles from the trailhead. Take a left fork on the main trail and continue up the canyon to the southwest. Soon the reservoir will come into view. To the right of the reservoir outlet are signs for Trail 707, which continues north, and for Trail 721, which proceeds west. Enjoy the tranquility and beauty of the reservoir before your return. Be careful with your footing on the loose gravel throughout most of the trail. You might consider visiting some of the attractions on the Air Force Academy grounds before or after the hike.

Stanley Canyon Reservoir.

PHOTO BY BILL STONE

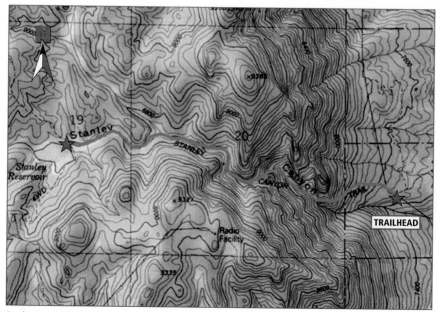

Stanley Canyon Reservoir.

6. American Lakes and Snow Lake

ROUND-TRIP DISTANCE	8.6 miles
HIKING TIME	Up in 125 minutes, down in 95 minutes
STARTING ELEVATION	9,800 feet
HIGHEST ELEVATION	11,516 feet
ELEVATION GAIN	2,076 feet (180 extra feet each way)
DIFFICULTY	Moderate
MAPS	Trails Illustrated, Rocky Mountain National Park, Number 200 Clark Peak 7.5 minute Chambers Lake 7.5 minute Fall River Pass 7.5 minute Mount Richthofen 7.5 minute Jackson County Number 4 Routt National Forest

COMMENT: Whatever you call them, the hike to the American Lakes (or Michigan Lakes), south of Cameron Pass, is one of the most beautiful hikes in the state. If you go in the second half of July, the wildflowers should delight you. The surrounding high peaks complement this special landscape. The trail signs consistently call the two lower lakes the American Lakes. The maps call them Michigan Lakes. They flow into the Michigan River.

GETTING THERE: From northwest of Fort Collins on U.S. 287, drive west on Colorado 14 for 57.8 miles to Cameron Pass. Then continue west on Colorado 14 for 2.4 miles and turn left onto an access road into the Colorado State Forest. (Admission fee required.) Follow this good dirt road for 0.6 mile. Then take the left fork and drive 0.9 mile further to a parking area on the right, at a road barrier.

THE HIKE: Begin east around the road barrier and past some extensive diggings on the left. Follow the overgrown road as it rises 1.2 miles to join the Michigan Ditch Road at a four-way intersection. The waters of the Michigan River will be flowing on your right. Continue straight (south-southeast) up the road, past a sign and register in open terrain. As you ascend, there are many clearings with great views of the peaks and upper slopes ahead. Cross a bridge and rise more steeply past timberline and enter one of the most beautiful basins you are likely to encounter. The green velvet tundra, flowers, and the mountains of the Never Summer Range greet you in all their glory.

The American Lakes from Snow Lake.

PHOTO BY RYAN LEWANDOWSKI

Continue by trail to the top of a grassy bench with the American Lakes on the right. The main trail continues straight and will eventually cross Thunder Pass. You take the narrow trail on the right (north-northwest), and soon traverse the northern edge of the two joined lakes. At the western end of these small lakes, locate a pole that marks the trail up to Snow Lake. This trail lies to the right of the creek, which flows into the American Lakes. After a short, steep climb, reach Snow Lake in a steep cirque below the Nokhu Crags to the west. The views to the north and east are special. Enjoy and return as you ascended.

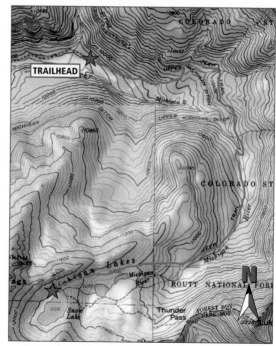

American Lakes and Snow Lake.

7. Cirque Lake and Emmaline Lake

ROUND-TRIP DISTANCE	10.8 miles
HIKING TIME	Up in 140 minutes, down in 120 minutes
STARTING ELEVATION	8,960 feet
HIGHEST ELEVATION	11,010 feet
ELEVATION GAIN	3,250 feet (includes an extra 600 feet each way)
DIFFICULTY	More difficult
MAPS	Trails Illustrated, Rocky Mountain National Park, Number 200 Comanche Peak 7.5 minute Pingree Park 7.5 minute Larimer County Number 3 Roosevelt National Forest

COMMENT: The trek to lovely Cirque and Emmaline Lakes traverses a remote area near the northeast corner of Rocky Mountain National Park in the Comanche Peak Wilderness. The trail becomes faint in its final segments before the lakes. Therefore, don't try this when snow covers the trail. The usual season for this outing is from July into very early October. This hike takes you along the edge of Pingree Park, which was ravaged by fire in July 1994. There is lots of flowing water and many log bridge crossings.

GETTING THERE: From the intersection with U.S. 287 northwest of Fort Collins, drive west on Colorado 14 up Poudre Canyon for 26.5 miles. Then turn left onto Larimer County Road 63 E. You will follow this good, main dirt road a total of 15.6 miles. En route to this point, go left at mile 4.2 from Colorado 14, and left again at mile 6.2. Go right at mile 7.8 and straight at mile 11.9. You will now be on Larimer Road 44 H. Keep right at mile 14.2, pass through some burnt timber and then turn right at mile 15.6, toward the Tom Bennett Campground. Take a right fork within 0.1 mile and a left fork within 150 yards farther. Here you meet the Emmaline Lake Trail sign. Follow this road on the left another 0.1 mile and park off the road. Four-wheel-drive is needed beyond this point. This rough road is blocked in another 0.4 mile.

THE HIKE: Walk up the rough road and after 0.4 mile pass around a closed gate into a clearing. Continue south-southwest with Pingree Park on the left and continue straight at two four-way intersections within 0.3 mile from the gate. Cross the first two of many log bridges and reach a sign and intersection, after 2.4 miles from your starting point. (Avoid the left fork, which goes

Cirque Lake below Comanche Peak.

PHOTO BY RYAN LEWANDOWSKI

to Mummy Pass in 5 miles.) Continue straight on the wide road, which leads 0.8 mile to Cirque Meadows and a sign. The view up into the high peaks from here is impressive. Continue to the right (north-northwest), cross a creek, and reenter the trees. Soon pass a wilderness sign and a trail register. It will be 2 more miles from here to an overview of beautiful Cirque Lake and a campground to the left of the lake. The last mile is steeper and the trail less distinct. Cairns mark the trail for another 0.1 mile from Cirque Lake north to larger Emmaline Lake. Comanche Peak and a rocky pinnacle lie to the west and Fall Mountain can be seen to the south. Relatively few hikers reach this gorgeous lake. Enjoy the grandeur before retracing your long ascent route back to your vehicle.

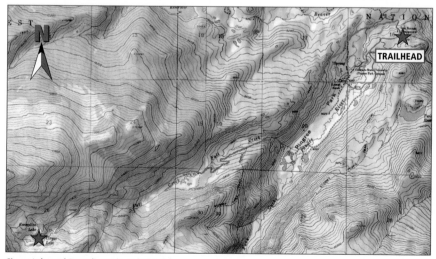

Cirque Lake and Emmaline Lake at lower left.

8. Browns Lake and Timberline Lake

ROUND-TRIP DISTANCE	8.4 miles
HIKING TIME	Out in 104 minutes, back in 112 minutes
STARTING ELEVATION	10,510 feet
HIGHEST ELEVATION	11,390 feet
ELEVATION GAIN	2,184 feet (includes 1,304 extra feet)
DIFFICULTY	Moderate
MAPS	Trails Illustrated, Poudre River/Cameron Pass, Number 112 Kinikinik 7.5 minute Comanche Peak 7.5 minute Larimer County Numbers 1 and 3 Roosevelt National Forest

COMMENT: The hike to Browns Lake and Timberline Lake is unusual in that the trailhead and the destination lie at the same elevation. The route enters the Comanche Peak Wilderness and crosses over two ridges before the final descent to the adjacent lakes. Bicycles and motorized vehicles are prohibited in the wilderness area and dogs must be kept on a leash. The season for this hike is from early July through October. This hike includes many fine vistas of the northern Colorado peaks.

GETTING THERE: From U.S. 287 northwest of Fort Collins, drive west on Colorado 14 for 26.0 miles and turn left onto the Pingree Park Road (Larimer County 63 E). After 4.2 miles on this good, wide, dirt road turn right onto the Crown Point Road. After 11.7 miles on the Crown Point Road, which is also a good gravel road, park on the right near trailhead signs. On the Crown Point Road, keep left at mile 1.5, right at mile 3.0, straight at mile 4.9, left at mile 6.2, and left again at mile 9.0. Generally, stay on the main road until you reach the trailhead.

THE HIKE: Cross the road and ascend to the south-southeast, past trailhead signs and a register on the good, gravel trail. Pass through intermittently level and semi-open forest before reaching the Comanche Peak Wilderness boundary sign and good vistas after 2.0 miles. Crown Point, a rocky knob, juts forth a few hundred yards above on your left. Continue down to the south across a large meadow. Then ascend another ridge before the descent to the lakes. On your way, cross an intersection with the Flowers Trail and a

Browns Lake.

PHOTO BY DAVE MULLER

cabin ruin on the right. Continue straight to several switchbacks that lead to Browns Lake on the right and smaller Timberline Lake 40 yards to the left. The trail continues to the south-southeast to Comanche Lake, Comanche Reservoir, and other connections.

The rocky cliffs on the west side of Browns Lake provide a rugged background. On your return, be ready for the good elevation gains back to the Crown Point area.

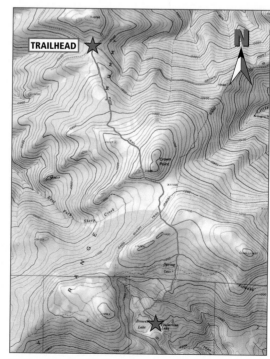

Browns Lake and Timberline Lake.

9. Ralph Price Reservoir

ROUND-TRIP DISTANCE	6.2 miles
HIKING TIME	Up in 72 minutes, down in 72 minutes
STARTING ELEVATION	5,940 feet
HIGHEST ELEVATION	6,620 feet
ELEVATION GAIN	1,630 feet (includes 950 extra feet)
DIFFICULTY	Moderate
MAPS	Trails Illustrated Number 100
	Lyons 7.5 minute
	Boulder County
	Roosevelt National Forest
	Button Rock Preserve

COMMENT: The Button Rock Reservoir has been renamed after the former Mayor of Longmont, Ralph Price. Here is a lovely hike to this lovely and large body of water, west of Lyons. Despite its proximity to front range Colorado population centers, this area is visited by relatively few hikers, but many fisherman.

GETTING THERE: From the west end of Lyons at the Intersection of U.S. 36 and Colorado 7, drive northwest on U.S. 36 for 4 miles and turn left onto County Road 80. Follow this very good dirt road for 2.7 miles to a road barrier at the Button Rock Nature Preserve and park on the left.

THE HIKE: Walk west through the gate and past a signboard. Bikes and horses are forbidden and dogs must be leashed on the roads in this preserve. No fee is required. Follow the wide dirt road past the Longmont Reservoir on the right and walk parallel to North Saint Vrain Creek, for 0.6 mile from the trailhead, to the sign for the Sleepy Lion Trail on the left. Hike southwest from here and leave the road. Ascend the trail into a high, open meadow with a striking and different view of Mount Meeker and Longs Peak to the west. Continue up and down through the trees to the high point of this trail at a fork at 6,620 feet. Take the right fork and continue south. (The left fork leads to Hall Ranch Park.) There are now good overlooks of the Button Rock Dam and the Ralph Price Reservoir. Beautiful rock formations abound on this hike. Ascend a brief rocky trail segment and then descend on an old road to the outlet below the dam and the end of the road that you left at the Sleepy Lion trailhead. Pick up the trail just west of and above the outflow of the reservoir and ascend steeply west to reach the dam crest and vast Ralph Price Reservoir. Smithy Mountain lies to the west-southwest and Button

Ralph Price Reservoir.

PHOTO BY CLIF REED

Rock Mountain to the northwest. A road continues west-northwest and passes a spillway before descending back to the main road. At the southeast end of the dam crest, a trail continues along the edge of the reservoir to an inlet at its southern shore. Explore and enjoy before retracing your route back to the trailhead. To shorten the return trip, you may wish to follow the road, which runs parallel to the creek for 1.6 miles back to the trailhead.

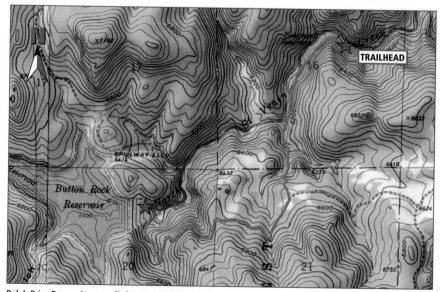

Ralph Price Reservoir was called Button Rock Reservoir.

10. Long Lake and Lake Isabelle

ROUND-TRIP DISTANCE	4.0 miles
HIKING TIME	Up in 47 minutes, down in 38 minutes
STARTING ELEVATION	10,520 feet
HIGHEST ELEVATION	10,920 feet
ELEVATION GAIN	654 feet (includes 254 extra feet each way)
DIFFICULTY	Easy
MAPS	Trails Illustrated, Indian Peaks/Gold Hill, Number 102 Ward 7.5 minute Boulder County Roosevelt National Forest

COMMENT: The Indian Peaks Wilderness is very popular for two main reasons: the scenery is gorgeous and the area is easily reached from Boulder and Denver. The usual hiking season here is from mid-July through October. This easy hike to Long Lake and Lake Isabelle brings you up a lovely valley along South Saint Vrain Creek, with several of the Indian Peaks rising above to the west.

GETTING THERE: From the town of Nederland, west of Boulder, drive northwest on Colorado 72 for 11.8 miles and turn left onto the Brainard Lake Road. After 2.6 miles, pass a fee station and continue 3.1 miles more and park at the Long Lake Trailhead. En route to this parking area, keep right at mile 4.7, left at mile 4.8, (from Colorado 72), drive along the right side of Brainard Lake, then turn right at mile 5.3 and left at mile 5.4 and quickly reach the parking area and trailhead.

Lake Isabelle.   PHOTO BY CLIF REED

Casting for the big one on Long Lake.

PHOTO BY KATHY PILLMORE

THE HIKE: Begin on the good trail to the southwest. After a few hundred yards keep right. (The Jean Lunning Trail goes to the left and encircles Long Lake.) Continue southwest with Long Lake on your left. After 1.0 mile from the trailhead, go right at a signed fork and ascend the valley another mile to beautiful Lake Isabelle. At the initial part of the lake, the Pawnee Pass Trail ascends to the right. Enjoy the grandeur of Lake Isabelle, with conical Navajo Peak and Apache Peak to the southwest, and the dramatic, jagged summit of Shoshoni Peak to the west-southwest. The trail continues up the basin to the Isabelle Glacier. For variety on your return, you can take the Jean Lunning Trail around Long Lake in a counterclockwise direction. To do so, take a sharp right at the sign and fork at the western end of Long Lake.

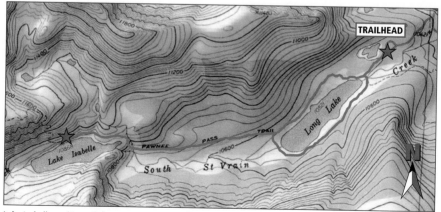

Lake Isabelle and Long Lake.

11. Diamond Lake

ROUND-TRIP DISTANCE	4.8 miles
HIKING TIME	Up in 68 minutes, down in 66 minutes
STARTING ELEVATION	10,180 feet
HIGHEST ELEVATION	10,950 feet
ELEVATION GAIN	1,550 feet (includes 780 extra feet)
DIFFICULTY	Moderate
MAPS	Trails Illustrated, Indian Peaks/Gold Hill, Number 102 East Portal 7.5 minute Monarch Lake 7.5 minute Boulder County Roosevelt National Forest

COMMENT: Any hike in the Indian Peaks Wilderness is a winner. The trail from Buckingham Campground is very popular and the parking areas are usually crowded. Arapaho Pass and South Arapaho Peak are other destinations that can be reached from this trailhead. The rushing waters of Middle Boulder Creek enhance this hike to a lovely lake.

GETTING THERE: From the intersection of Colorado 119 and Colorado 72 in Nederland, drive south on Colorado 119 for 0.6 mile and turn right onto Boulder Road 130. Turn your mileage to zero. Keep right at mile 0.8 and again at mile 1.9. Drive through the town of Eldora and up the unpaved road beyond. Keep right at mile 4.1 and continue up the right fork to parking and road end at mile 8.2.

THE HIKE: Begin to the north from the trailhead signs at the upper parking area. The good trail curves west with intermittent vistas as it climbs to a signed fork at mile 1.3. Take the left fork to the west, as the other trail ascends up the valley toward Arapaho Pass. Gradually descend into the thick forest for 0.7 mile to a bridge crossing of the North Fork of Middle Boulder Creek. A scenic waterfall can be viewed 50 yards upstream. Continue the final 0.6 mile up to a signed trail fork in a clearing. Go right (south) 100 yards to the diamond-shaped lake and several nearby campsites. The Continental Divide lies to the west and towering South Arapaho Peak can be seen through the trees to the north-northwest.

Diamond Lake and South Arapaho Peak.

PHOTO BY DAVE MULLER

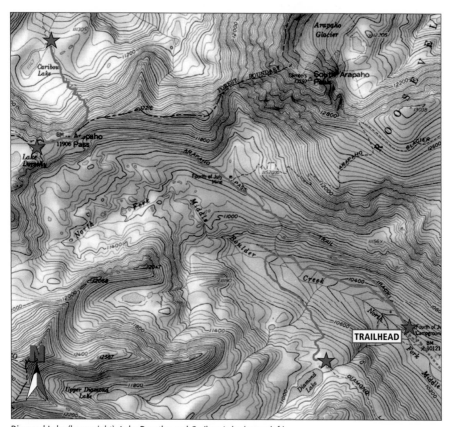

Diamond Lake (lower right), Lake Dorothy, and Caribou Lake (upper left).

12. Lake Dorothy and Caribou Lake

ROUND-TRIP DISTANCE	3.3 miles up to Lake Dorothy, 1.3 miles over and down to Caribou Lake, Caribou Lake to trailhead in 4 miles, total 8.6 miles
HIKING TIME	Up to Lake Dorothy in 95 minutes, over and down to Caribou Lake in 32 minutes, Caribou Lake back to trailhead in 95 minutes, total 222 minutes.
STARTING ELEVATION	10,180 feet
HIGHEST ELEVATION	12,061 feet
ELEVATION GAIN	2,950 feet (includes 1,069 extra feet)
DIFFICULTY	Moderate
MAPS	Trails Illustrated, Indian Peaks/Gold Hill, Number 102 East Portal 7.5 minute Monarch Lake 7/5 minute Boulder County Grand County Number 4 Roosevelt National Forest Arapaho National Forest

COMMENT: This trek to two scenic lakes in the Indian Peaks Wilderness is full of beautiful vistas. The route up the valley on a fine trail provides great viewing of the nearby peaks and the valley below. Two trails branch off from the Arapaho Pass Trail before the pass: one to Diamond Lake and the second to the Arapaho Glacier and South Arapaho Peak. At mile 2, you pass the ruins of the Fourth of July Mine.

Due to its great natural beauty and proximity to Boulder, this is a very popular hiking area. Consider going during the week or making a very early start. Bikes are forbidden on the trails and dogs must be leashed.

GETTING THERE: From the junction of Colorado 72 and Colorado 119 in Nederland, drive south on Colorado 119 for 0.6 mile and turn right (west). Drive 9.1 miles on this main road through the town of Eldora to trailhead parking near the Fourth of July Campground. En route to this parking area, keep right at mile 1.5 and again at mile 4.9 from Colorado 119. Keep left at mile 7.7 and stay on the main road. Regular cars can reach the parking area.

THE HIKE: Begin north-northeast from the trailhead sign. Ascend to the west and reach a signed fork after 1.3 miles. Keep to the right, since the left trail descends to Diamond Lake. After another 0.7 mile, take the left fork, with

Lake Dorothy and Mount Neva.   PHOTO BY DAVID HITE

the Fourth of July Mine ruins and the trail to the Arapaho Glacier on your right. Ascend on a good, rocky, direct trail for the final mile to Arapaho Pass, at another signed fork. Take the left fork, which leads to Caribou Pass, for 0.3 mile and leave the trail to reach lovely Lake Dorothy on the left at the foot of Mount Neva. After enjoying this lake, retrace your route back to the last fork at Arapaho Pass and now go northeast by trail to a rocky wind shelter on the ridge before descending north for a final mile to serene Caribou Lake, lying beneath Satanta Peak. The good trail passes to the right of the lake and continues down to Coyote Park and Monarch Lake. Leave the trail near the lake and walk 50 yards to its banks. Refresh your spirit and enjoy viewing the impressive peaks to the north and northeast before the 4 mile return to the trailhead. The season for this outing will usually be from mid-June through October with late July offering a wildflower bonanza.

SIDEBAR: Pine Beetles

There are several types of bark beetles that attack pine, blue spruce, ash, and elm trees. A prevalent theory about why these beetles have become so numerous and destructive says that a prolonged winter freeze of several days in the range of −22° to −44° is needed to kill the beetles and spare the trees. Such prolonged freezes have been occurring less often over the last ten years.

SEE MAP PAGE 37

13. Jasper Lake

ROUND-TRIP DISTANCE	10 miles
HIKING TIME	Up in 140 minutes, down in 120 minutes
STARTING ELEVATION	9,000 feet
HIGHEST ELEVATION	10,852 feet (above the lake)
ELEVATION GAIN	2,042 feet (includes 190 extra feet)
DIFFICULTY	More difficult
MAPS	Trails Illustrated, Indian Peaks/Gold Hill, Number 102 Nederland 7.5 minute East Portal 7.5 minute Boulder County Roosevelt National Forest

COMMENT: Many good hikes begin at the site of the former town of Hessie, west of Nederland and Eldora. This hike ascends a beautiful valley with many high peaks and abundant rushing water to please the eye and ear. Most of this route lies within the very popular Indian Peaks Wilderness.

GETTING THERE: From the junction with Colorado 72 in Nederland, drive south on Colorado 119 for 0.6 mile and turn right (west). Keep right at 1.5 miles and drive through the town of Eldora. Continue up the dirt road after passing through the town and reach a fork and a sign after 4.9 miles from Colorado 119. Descend the left fork for 0.2 mile and park by a corral and a sign at the site of the former town of Hessie.

THE HIKE: Begin hiking to the west on the road from the Hessie town site. After 0.25 mile at road end, cross a bridge at the Hessie trailhead. (Only higher clearance vehicles can drive this far.) In another 0.2 mile, keep straight on the main road at a four-way intersection. After several hundred more yards, leave the road and go right at a fork and a sign just before a bridge over the South Fork of Middle Boulder Creek. Follow this good trail southwest up into the basin. Pass a wilderness sign and in 0.7 mile from the sign take a right (northwest) fork. (The left fork crosses the creek and leads back to the Woodland Lake Trail.) In another 0.25 mile, leave the road and take the footpath up to the right, which is north-northwest. Keep on the main trail going generally northwest for another 2.25 miles to a fork. Go left another 0.5 mile to Jasper Lake or Reservoir. (The right fork goes to Diamond Lake.) The lake is fairly large, with a metal storage shack at its east

D.J. Inman at Jasper Lake.

end. Devils Thumb Pass and Devils Thumb lie above to the west-southwest. The trail continues in that direction one mile further to Devils Thumb Lake and another mile to the pass.

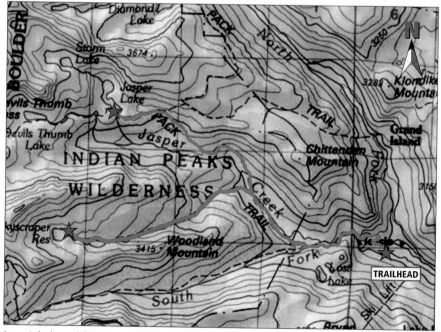

Jasper Lake (upper left), Skyscraper Reservoir and Woodland Lake (lower left).

14. Woodland Lake and Skyscraper Reservoir

ROUND-TRIP DISTANCE	11.2 miles
HIKING TIME	Up to Woodland Lake in 152 minutes, 24 minutes more to Skyscraper Reservoir, down in 137 minutes (Total 313 minutes)
STARTING ELEVATION	9,000 feet
HIGHEST ELEVATION	11,300 feet
ELEVATION GAIN	3,140 feet (includes 420 extra feet each way)
DIFFICULTY	More difficult
MAPS	Trails Illustrated, Indian Peaks/Gold Hill, Number 102 Nederland 7.5 minute East Portal 7.5 minute Boulder County Roosevelt National Forest

COMMENT: The contrasting names of these two lakes is significant. The lower, Woodland Lake, is bucolic and invites the camper to pitch a tent. The upper, Skyscraper Reservoir, is more severe, with less open, green areas and a man-made dam at its outlet. Both are worthwhile destinations within the Indian Peaks Wilderness, one of the garden spots of Colorado.

GETTING THERE: From the junction of Colorado 119 and Colorado 72 in Nederland, drive south on Colorado 119 for 0.6 mile, and turn right toward the town of Eldora. Keep right at 1.5 miles from Colorado 119 and stay on the main road as it continues through Eldora. Ascend the dirt road to a junction and signs at mile 4.9 from Colorado 119. Some cars park here. But, with reasonable clearance, you can descend the left fork for 0.3 mile and park on the right at the former town site of Hessie.

THE HIKE: From the Hessie townsite, begin west-northwest up the rough road. Quickly cross a bridge at the Hessie trailhead. (Some vehicles can come this far.) After another 100 yards, keep straight at a four-way trail intersection and wind up the valley as you emerge from the forest. At mile 1.2, cross a bridge at trail signs. The rushing waters of the South Fork of Middle Boulder Creek pass impressively beneath you. Continue up the road with the creek now on your right. 200 yards from the bridge, avoid the left fork to Lost Lake. 0.2 mile further, the trail splits again. The left fork continues to

Woodland Lake.

PHOTO BY CLIF REED

King Lake. You take the trail on the right and proceed west to enter the wilderness at signs after crossing an open meadow. Take a left fork (southwest) at an unmarked junction, after another 0.25 mile. With the creek on your right, reach a signed fork at mile 2.3 of your hike. The right trail crosses Jasper Creek en route to Jasper Lake and Devils Thumb Lake. You continue left and at mile 2.9 finally cross the creek, which flows down from Woodland Lake. Then, ascend a clearing before reentering the woods for the final 2.2 miles to inviting Woodland Lake.

To reach Skyscraper Reservoir, lying to the west, continue by trail to the west-northwest. After 0.2 mile, the trail becomes faint as you traverse a marshy area and cross the creek at a narrow channel before regaining a brief clear trail. You now have two choices: continue on the trail until it fades away and then work your way up and around the left side of the rocky buttress, which overlooks the reservoir; or note the cascading water flowing down from the reservoir and work your way to it, around the greener areas to the right of the outflow. Drink in the grandeur before your lengthy return through this lovely wilderness.

SEE MAP PAGE 41

15. Coney Lake

ROUND-TRIP DISTANCE	15.2 miles
HIKING TIME	Up in 175 minutes, down in 140 minutes
STARTING ELEVATION	8,675 feet
HIGHEST ELEVATION	10,560 feet
ELEVATION GAIN	3,425 feet (includes 770 extra feet each way)
DIFFICULTY	More difficult
MAPS	Trails Illustrated, Indian Peaks, Number 102 Allens Park 7.5 minute Ward 7.5 minute Boulder County Roosevelt National Forest

COMMENT: The magical Indian Peaks Wilderness offers many lovely hiking destinations. Some of the best are its lakes. Coney Lake is not easy to reach, but the scenic wall of peaks to its south makes it especially worth the effort. A coney is a small mountain animal, also called a pika. Due to the necessary creek crossings, the best time for this hike is in September and October.

GETTING THERE: From Nederland, drive north on Colorado 72 for 17.5 miles and turn left onto the side road to Camp Dick. Follow this road through a campground for 1.2 miles from Colorado 72 to the beginning of the rough four-wheel-drive, Middle Saint Vrain Creek Road, and park. (Many four-wheel-drive vehicles will have trouble with this old mining road.)

THE HIKE: Begin hiking up the very rough, gradual road to the west. Continue straight as the Buchanan Pass Trail goes to the right after 0.1 mile. After almost 1 mile, pass the sign to Timberline Falls on the right. (A short, poor side trail brings you to an overlook of the rushing water.) Continue up the road another 3 miles to a sign and intersection. Ascend steep Coney Cutoff Road on the left for another mile to the Coney Flats trailhead, which also can be reached from Beaver Reservoir. Take the trail leading west from the left side of the trailhead sign and reach a signed fork in another 0.25 mile. Go left (west-southwest) across open terrain before entering the trees and making two significant crossings of Coney Creek. Follow the trail as it curves right after 1.6 miles from the fork and passes between two small ponds. The trail briefly becomes faint, but continues above the ponds on the right, up the valley. Ascend to a grassy, rocky bench and soon reach the final short

Coney Lake.

PHOTO BY DAVE MULLER

descent to Coney Lake, where the trail ends. (Upper Coney Lake is an easy trek further up the basin.) Mount Audubon looms impressively above to the south-southeast and Paiute Peak to the south-southwest.

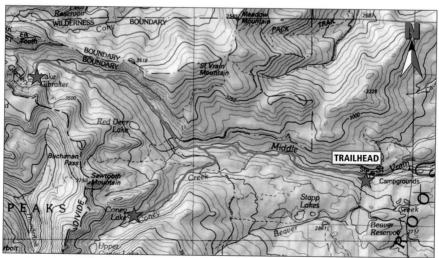

Coney Lake (lower left), Lake Gibraltar (upper left).

16. Lake Gibraltar

ROUND-TRIP DISTANCE	16.4 miles
HIKING TIME	Up in 234 minutes, down in 178 minutes
STARTING ELEVATION	8,670 feet
HIGHEST ELEVATION	11,190 feet
ELEVATION GAIN	3,640 feet (includes 560 extra feet each way)
DIFFICULTY	Most difficult
MAPS	Trails Illustrated, Indian Peaks/Gold Hill, Number 102 Allens Park 7.5 minute Isolation Peak 7.5 minute Boulder County Roosevelt National Forest

COMMENT: The long hike to Lake Gibraltar leads to a lovely basin beneath the Saint Vrain Glacier in the Indian Peaks Wilderness. The length of the hike and the lack of other destinations in the area explain the relatively light use of this beautiful trail. There are three crossings of Middle Saint Vrain Creek in the upper third of this hike. I would, therefore, recommend this outing after mid-July, when the water level is lower.

GETTING THERE: Drive north on Colorado 72 from Nederland for 17.5 miles and turn left into Camp Dick. Avoid the campsites and drive 1.2 miles from Colorado 72 to a parking area where the road to the west becomes very rocky and rough.

THE HIKE: The hike begins west on the rough road leading from the parking area. Within 100 yards, take a right fork and descend northwest on the Buchanan Pass Trail. Cross Middle Saint Vrain Creek by bridge and ascend west up the valley on a good trail for 4 miles to a signed junction with a

Lake Gibraltar.　　　　PHOTO BY FRANK BURZYNSKI

Lake Gibraltar.

PHOTO BY FRANK BURZYNSKI

wide, rocky road. (At one unmarked fork keep right.) At the road continue to the right (southwest). After another 0.5 mile, pass the Indian Peaks Wilderness boundary and the Saint Vrain Mountain Trail on the right. Continue northwest up the gradual road. You are now on the Saint Vrain Glacier Trail. This is a very scenic valley with several of the Indian Peaks on the horizon.

After 0.9 mile from the wilderness boundary, take the right fork at a sign. (The left fork leads to Red Deer Lake and Buchanan Pass.) Rise higher in the valley and pass some wooden remnants on your left. You soon will make a series of creek crossings. Three of these cross Middle Saint Vrain Creek on logs. Follow the good trail. The terrain becomes more open and full of flowers as you ascend. When the trail becomes less distinct, cairns guide you. Eventually you reach the outflow of Lake Gibraltar. Follow the trail with this creek always on your right. Ascend a grassy basin and pass the final cairn. It is clockwise another 200 yards southeast and south and over a final boulder field before you reach somber Lake Gibraltar, beneath some of the Saint Vrain Glacier. Elk Tooth is the peak to the northwest and Ogalalla Peak lies to the west-northwest. Enjoy this striking destination in this remote cul-de-sac before the long walk back.

SEE MAP PAGE 45

17. James Peak Lake and Little Echo Lake

ROUND-TRIP DISTANCE	Trailhead to James Peak Lake 2.5 miles, James Peak Lake to Little Echo Lake 0.9 miles, Little Echo Lake back to trailhead 2.6 miles (Total loop 6.0 miles)
HIKING TIME	Trailhead to James Peak Lake in 60 minutes, James Peak Lake to Little Echo Lake in 35 minutes, Little Echo Lake back to trailhead in 54 minutes (Total 149 minutes)
STARTING ELEVATION	11,180 feet
HIGHEST ELEVATION	11,570 feet
ELEVATION GAIN	1,305 feet (includes 915 extra feet)
DIFFICULTY	Moderate
MAPS	Trails Illustrated, Winter Park/Central City/Rollins Pass, Number 103 Empire 7.5 minute Gilpin County Roosevelt National Forest

COMMENT: James Peak Lake and Little Echo Lake are surrounded by lovely scenery and reached by well-marked trails at the head of Mammoth Gulch. Yet they lie in an out-of-the-way area and experience relatively little use. This route is mostly above timberline and the vistas are wonderful.

GETTING THERE: From Rollinsville on Colorado 119, south of Nederland, drive west on the good, dirt Rollins Pass Road. Keep straight at mile 0.8 from Colorado 119 and at mile 5.1, just past Tolland, take the left fork up Mammoth Gulch. From the Rollins Pass Road, keep straight at mile 0.1, left at the four-way intersection at mile 1.7, straight at mile 2.3, again at mile 3.6, and again at mile 4.8. Stay on Road 353. Take the right fork at mile 5.1 and park near the fork at mile 5.5. Regular cars should be able to come this far but four-wheel-drive is required past this point.

THE HIKE: From your parking area at the fork in the road, begin hiking up the right fork in a westerly direction. After 1.4 miles on the rough road you reach a sharp bend in the road to the left and the James Peak Lake trailhead sign. Descend this trail to the west-southwest and in 0.7 mile you will reach signs at a fork. The left trail leads to James Peak Lake and the right fork goes to Little Echo Lake, and beyond to Rogers Pass on the Continental Divide.

James Peak Lake.   PHOTO BY DAVE MULLER

Go left past some tarns and waterfalls on your right and in 0.6 mile from the fork reach James Peak Lake, with impressive James Peak above to the west-southwest. An abandoned cabin lies near the lake. To continue this loop hike, return by trail to the fork and descend left below timberline, cross the creek, and then follow the trail up over tundra to serene Little Echo Lake. The trail continues along the right side of the lake and rises to the Continental Divide and beyond. Return back to the fork to James Peak Lake, go left and ascend the 500 feet back to the road and the final 1.4 miles to reach your car.

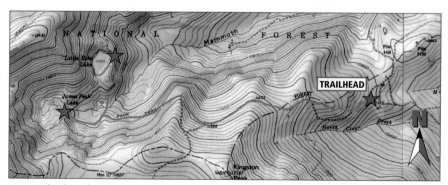

James Peak Lake and Little Echo Lake.

18. The Crater Lakes

ROUND-TRIP DISTANCE	7 miles
HIKING TIME	Up in 106 minutes, down in 78 minutes
STARTING ELEVATION	9,200 feet
HIGHEST ELEVATION	11,035 feet
ELEVATION GAIN	2,075 feet (includes 120 extra feet each way)
DIFFICULTY	Moderate
MAPS	Trails Illustrated, Winter Park/Central City/Rollins Pass, Number 103 East Portal 7.5 minute Gilpin County Roosevelt National Forest

COMMENT: The hike to the Crater Lakes is one of the better, flowing-water outings in the state. The trail initially parallels South Boulder Creek southwest of the Moffat Tunnel. After crossing creeks from the Forest Lakes and the Arapaho Lakes, a side trail rises steeply to several high lakes and lots of cascading water, especially just below the highest of the Crater Lakes. Of the many lakes in this area, the Crater Lakes, in my opinion, provide the best hike. Try this outing in late June or July when the streams are not too high.

GETTING THERE: From Colorado 119 at Rollinsville, south of Nederland, drive west on Road 149 toward Rollins Pass and set your mileage to zero. Follow the wide, unpaved, main road through Tolland at mile 4.9 and past the road to Apex on the left, at mile 5.1. Cross the railroad tracks and go left at a T and leave Road 149, which goes to the right at mile 7.2. At mile 8.0, park in the large open area at road end, near the Moffat Tunnel. Regular cars can easily reach this parking area.

Upper Crater Lake. PHOTO BY DAVID HITE

Lower Crater Lake.

PHOTO BY DAVID HITE

THE HIKE: Proceed to the south-southwest from the parking area, cross the railroad tracks, and cross a bridge with the Moffat Tunnel on your right. Follow the wide, clear trail past a cabin and signboard. Soon, cross a series of wooden bridges and follow the main trail as it ascends alongside South Boulder Creek on the left. After 1.2 miles, pass through an open meadow with two cabin ruins on the left. A side trail near three wooden poles at the beginning of this meadow ascends to the Arapaho Lakes and the Forest Lakes. 0.6 mile farther brings you to a side trail on the left and a cairn-marked trail on the right, just before a small creek descends from the right. Leave the main trail and ascend this right fork to the north-northwest. This rough trail becomes quite steep as it ascends into the Crater Lakes basin. Follow the trail as it passes between the two middle Crater Lakes and then along the left side of the lake on the right. The trail then ascends before reaching the creek that supplies this lake. This steep trail passes to the right of a rocky peak and encounters beautiful waterfalls and cascades emanating from the upper Crater Lakes. Shortly before the final steep section, you cross the outflow creek and ascend first to a smaller lake and then the final, larger, upper Crater Lake, just below tree line. The Continental Divide lies above. On your return, you may wish to take a side trip to the lowest Crater Lake, which is supplied by the two middle lakes.

SEE MAP PAGE 53

19. Arapaho Lake

ROUND-TRIP DISTANCE	7.4 miles
HIKING TIME	Up in 145 minutes, down in 96 minutes
STARTING ELEVATION	9,200 feet
HIGHEST ELEVATION	11,140 feet
ELEVATION GAIN	2,100 feet (includes 80 extra feet each way)
DIFFICULTY	Moderate
MAPS	Trails Illustrated, Winter Park/Central City/Rollins Pass, Number 103 East Portal 7.5 minute Gilpin County Roosevelt National Forest

COMMENT: If you like hikes with lots of gushing water nearby, this outing to Arapaho Lake is for you. Due to several creek crossings, the better time for this hike is the second half of the hiking season (i.e., after early August.) The Arapaho Lakes are usually referred to in the plural. The trail leads to the largest one, which will be referred to as Arapaho Lake. You may wish to explore some of the other, smaller, Arapaho Lakes nearby. There are no signs after the trailhead and many fallen logs cross the trail. Beware of trying to reach the Arapaho Lakes by trail from the Forest Lakes. Some maps show a trail but it is difficult to find.

GETTING THERE: From Rollinsville on Colorado 119, south of Nederland, drive west on Road 149 toward Rollins Pass and the East Portal of the Moffat Tunnel. Follow the wide, unpaved road through Tolland, at mile 4.9, and past the road to Apex on the left at mile 5.1. Cross the railroad tracks and go left at mile 7.2. (The Moffat Road leads to the right.) Park at mile 8.0 in the large open area at road end, just east of the Moffat Tunnel. Regular cars can easily reach this parking area.

THE HIKE: From the parking area, walk toward the Moffat Tunnel and cross the tracks by bridge on the left to gain the trail. Enter the trees and follow the old road with South Boulder Creek on your left. Pass some old cabins and reach a fork in a large meadow at mile 1.2. Turn right here and ascend west-northwest across a creek and up an old road to another, more formidable, creek crossing on boulders. Continue almost another mile to a wooden bridge crossing of Arapaho Creek. The trail becomes steeper and,

Arapaho Lake.

PHOTO BY DAVE MULLER

after a few hundred yards, you reach the confluence of two creeks descending from the left. Ascend the trail to the left between these creeks and steeply rise amid rushing water to enter a broad, open valley. The trail continues straight and then curves up to the left to reach Arapaho Lake, under the Continental Divide. Count your blessings, refresh, and relax before returning by your ascent trail.

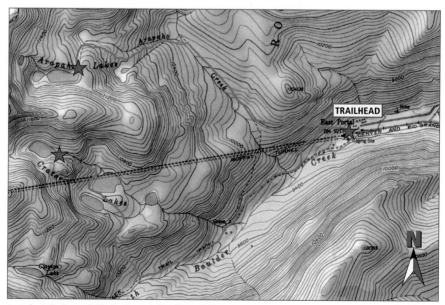

Arapaho Lake (upper left), the Crater Lakes (lower left).

53

20. The Dry Lakes

ROUND-TRIP DISTANCE	8.8 miles
HIKING TIME	Up in 164 minutes, down in 105 minutes
STARTING ELEVATION	9,020 feet
HIGHEST ELEVATION	11,865 feet
ELEVATION GAIN	3,315 feet (includes 235 extra feet each way)
DIFFICULTY	More difficult
MAPS	Trails Illustrated Number 138 Horn Peak 7.5 minute Custer County Number 1 San Isabel National Forest

COMMENT: The Rainbow Trail runs for many miles along the eastern flank of the Sangre de Cristo Mountains, west of Westcliffe and Silver Cliff. A series of trails begins from the Rainbow Trail and ascends the valleys to the west. The trail to the Dry Lakes is one of these. It follows Dry Creek steeply up into a gorgeous high basin encircled by Little Horn Peak, Fluted Peak, and Horn Peak. Bicycles are not allowed on this trail. The usual season is from early July until mid-October.

GETTING THERE: From the intersection of Colorado 96 and Colorado 67 in Westcliffe, drive south on Colorado 67 for 6.6 miles and turn right onto Road 130. Drive 6.6 more miles on this road, where it ends at the Horn Creek Ranch. Turn right here and drive 0.3 mile further to the Horn Creek trailhead and park.

THE HIKE: From the Horn Creek Trailhead, take either of two trails to the southwest and reach the Rainbow Trail after 0.3 mile. Take the right fork and descend to the west-northwest for 0.1 mile to the sign for the Dry Creek Trail. Leave the Rainbow Trail and ascend to your left (south). Quickly pass a signboard and register on the left and climb steeply with Dry Creek on your right. After 1 mile through the forest from the Rainbow Trail, cross Dry Creek on some logs and continue your steep ascent. Eventually pass through some aspen mixed with the evergreens and the rushing waters of Dry Creek, now on your left. The trail becomes more gradual before getting steeper again after a Sangre de Cristo Wilderness sign. Continue upward past timberline to a grassy bench with the four Dry Lakes beyond in a magnificent basin in the midst of three major peaks. A faint trail leads around the right

Dry Lake Number Two and Fluted Peak.

PHOTO BY DAVE MULLER

side of Dry Lake Number One for 0.3 mile and ends at the second and larger lake. Two smaller lakes lie farther up into the basin. Enjoy such beauty before your trek back down to the Rainbow Trail and the trailhead.

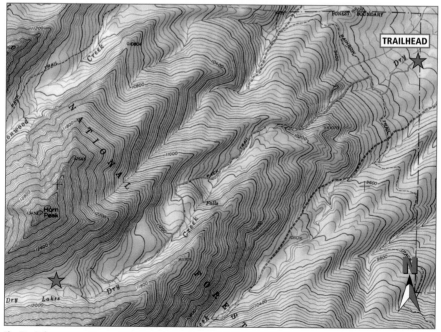

The Dry Lakes.

21. Bierstadt Lake

ROUND-TRIP DISTANCE	Trailhead to Lake Bierstadt, 1.8 miles; loop around Lake, 0.8 miles; return to trailhead 1.6 miles (Total 4.2 miles)
HIKING TIME	Up to Lake Bierstadt in 49 minutes, loop around Lake in 20 minutes, down in 34 minutes (Total 103 minutes)
STARTING ELEVATION	8,640 feet
HIGHEST ELEVATION	9,425 feet
ELEVATION GAIN	900 feet (includes 115 extra feet)
DIFFICULTY	Easy
MAPS	Trails Illustrated, Rocky Mountain National Park, Number 200, or Longs Peak, Number 301 McHenrys Peak 7.5 minute Longs Peak 7.5 minute Larimer County Number 3

COMMENT: There are several paths to beautiful Bierstadt Lake, which is named after the famous German artist, Alfred Bierstadt. This route offers easier trailhead parking and a short but steep trek to the lake and the trail around it. There are good mountain views from the lake and numerous aspen trees over the lower half of the hike. For all Rocky Mountain National Park trails, bicycles, pets, and guns are forbidden.

GETTING THERE: From the Beaver Meadows Entrance to Rocky Mountain National Park, on the west side of Estes Park, drive west 0.2 mile, then turn left onto the Bear Lake Road. Follow this paved road for 4.9 miles and turn right into the large shuttle bus parking area. Park near the trailhead at the southwest edge of the lot, within 150 yards of the Bear Lake Road. Note: another, small, Bierstadt Lake trailhead parking area lies further to the south on the Bear Lake Road.

THE HIKE: Start to the southwest from the trailhead signs and ascend a steep, rocky trail. After 0.2 mile, take the right fork at signs and continue up to the northwest. Soon you will be on an open slope with wonderful views across the valley on your left. After some more steep climbing, you reach a signed fork on level terrain and proceed to the right (north-northwest). Within 100 yards, take the trail on the left and walk south 60 yards to Bierstadt Lake. Longs Peak towers above to the south-southeast and Hallett Peak is to the southwest. For the trail around the lake, return to your last fork and

Bierstadt Lake.

PHOTO BY KIEFER THOMAS

continue left (west), and circle the lake in a counterclockwise direction through the trees.

The scenery is better as you move away from the lake. Take a series of three left forks at well-marked trail junctions and arrive back at the intersection where you reached the level terrain. Descend to the east back to your trailhead.

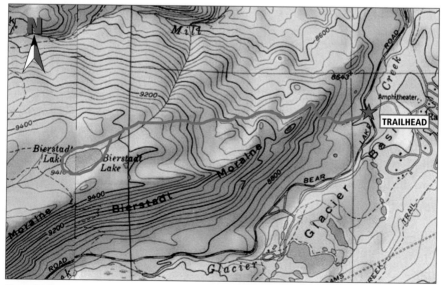

Bierstadt Lake.

22. Fern Lake and Odessa Lake

ROUND-TRIP DISTANCE	9 miles
HIKING TIME	Up in 120 minutes, down in 98 minutes
STARTING ELEVATION	8,150 feet
HIGHEST ELEVATION	10,020 feet
ELEVATION GAIN	2,700 feet (includes 415 extra feet each way)
DIFFICULTY	Moderate
MAPS	Trails Illustrated, Rocky Mountain National Park, Number 200 or Longs Peak, Number 301 McHenrys Peak 7.5 minute Larimer County Number 4

COMMENT: Hiking to Odessa Lake brings you to one especially beautiful area after the other. In order, these are: The Arch Rocks, The Pool, Fern Falls, Fern Lake, and then extraordinary Odessa Lake itself. Since this all lies within Rocky Mountain National Park, an entrance fee is required. Pets and bicycles are forbidden on these fine trails. Odessa Lake is named after the daughter of an early settler in this area.

GETTING THERE: From the Beaver Meadows entrance to Rocky Mountain National Park, west of Estes Park, drive west 0.2 mile and turn left onto the Bear Lake Road. After 1.3 miles on the Bear Lake Road, turn right into Moraine Park. Follow this road 2.6 more miles and park at the end of the road at the Fern Lake trailhead. En route to the trailhead, take two left forks on the Moraine Park Road. Regular cars can readily reach this parking area.

THE HIKE: Start on foot to the west from the trailhead signboard. Follow the trail, with the Big Thompson River on your left. After 0.75 mile the trail passes through several huge boulders, known as the Arch Rocks. In almost another mile you will reach The Pool, a lovely stretch of the Big Thompson River. At a sign ascend the right fork. (The left trail goes to Cub Lake and Mill Creek Basin.) The trail rises more steeply almost another mile to dramatic Fern Falls on the left. Continue upward through pine forest another 1.1 miles to a sign at a trail intersection. The right fork leads to Spruce Lake. You go left, however, to quickly reach scenic Fern Lake, with a ranger cabin on the right. Continue around the left side of the lake, on the trail. After 0.5 mile from Fern Lake, go right at a trail intersection and hike along the outflow from Odessa Lake for 0.2 mile to reach Odessa Lake. The

Fern Lake.

PHOTO BY JAY FELL

beauty here is special. Little Matterhorn looms above to the southwest. Notchtop Mountain can be seen to the south. Grace Falls is halfway up to the ridge to the south-southwest. There should be no problems on your return if you take the proper forks.

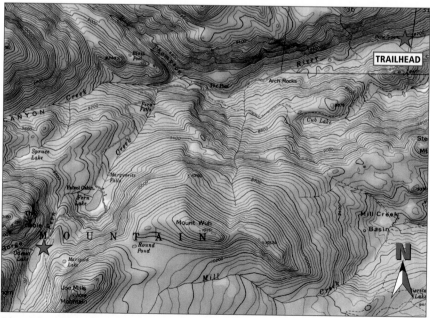

Odessa Lake and Fern Lake.

23. Lake Haiyaha

ROUND-TRIP DISTANCE	4.2 miles
HIKING TIME	Up in 60 minutes, down in 50 minutes
STARTING ELEVATION	9,475 feet
HIGHEST ELEVATION	10,240 feet
ELEVATION GAIN	935 feet (includes 85 extra feet each way)
DIFFICULTY	Easy
MAPS	Trails Illustrated, Rocky Mountain National Park, Number 200 or Longs Peak, Number 301 McHenrys Peak 7.5 minute Larimer County Number 3 Roosevelt National Forest

COMMENT: The Hike from Bear Lake to Lake Haiyaha is loaded with beautiful scenery and passes by two intervening lakes. The trail is very well marked and it's a good outing for families. Bikes and dogs are forbidden on the trails of Rocky Mountain National Park. Once called Rainbow Lake, it was renamed after a Native American word for rocks.

GETTING THERE: From the Beaver Meadows entrance to Rocky Mountain National Park, at the western edge of Estes Park, drive into the park for 0.2 miles and turn left onto the Bear Lake Road. Drive 9.0 miles on this good paved road until it ends at a large parking lot. Park here.

THE HIKE: Walk west-northwest from the Bear Lake parking area and in 100 yards take the left fork just before Bear Lake is reached. (Beautiful Bear Lake is well worth a side trip and has an encircling trail.) In another 100 yards, reach the Emerald Lake Trailhead and take a right fork heading south toward Nymph Lake. After 0.5 mile, pass lovely Nymph Lake on your left and, after another 0.5 mile of ascent, reach a sign at a fork. Dream Lake is 0.1 mile to the right and well worth the trip. Take the left fork for the final 1.1 miles to Lake Haiyaha. Shortly before the lake a trail from Glacier Gorge Junction enters from the left. The final 100 yards to Lake Haiyaha requires some easy scrambling over boulders. The trail ends at the lake and shoreline boulders.

Lake Haiyaha.   PHOTO BY JAY FELL

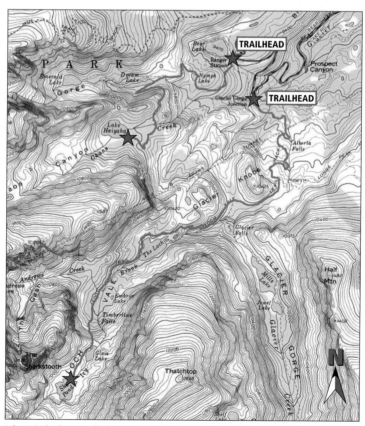

Lake Haiyaha (top route), Sky Pond, Lake of Glass, and The Loch (bottom route).

24. The Loch, Lake of Glass, and Sky Pond

ROUND-TRIP DISTANCE	9.8 miles
HIKING TIME	Up in 148 minutes, down in 116 minutes
STARTING ELEVATION	9,160 feet
HIGHEST ELEVATION	10,900 feet
ELEVATION GAIN	2,440 feet (includes an extra 350 feet each way)
DIFFICULTY	Moderate
MAPS	Trails Illustrated, Rocky Mountain National Park, Number 200 or Longs Peak, Number 301 McHenrys Peak 7.5 minute Larimer County Number 3

COMMENT: Visitors come from all over the world to see Rocky Mountain National Park. This classic hike to three glorious lakes exemplifies why the park is so renowned. The well-marked trail provides a series of highlights. These are, in the order of appearance: Alberta Falls, The Loch, Timberline Falls, the Lake of Glass, and Sky Pond. The latter two lakes lie in a steep, rocky amphitheater beneath the Continental Divide. A park fee is required. Vehicles and dogs are forbidden on the trails within the park.

GETTING THERE: From the Beaver Meadows entrance to Rocky Mountain National Park (west of Estes Park) drive into the park for 0.2 mile and turn left onto the Bear Lake Road. Keep left at 1.3 miles and stay on the Bear Lake Road another 6.7 miles and park on the left at the Glacier Gorge trailhead parking area. (If the lot is full, drive up the road and park in the massive Bear Lake lot. A trail connects Bear Lake with the Glacier Gorge Trailhead.)

THE HIKE: Begin south-southwest and follow the clear trail past a left fork to Sprague Lake and up to another signed fork after 0.3 mile from the trailhead. Go left here toward Mills Lake and The Loch. After 0.9 mile from the trailhead, pass the roaring waters of Alberta Falls on the left. Stay on the excellent trail another 0.6 mile and again take a right fork at a trail sign. Descend slightly another 0.4 mile and go right at a fork, as the left fork leads to Mills Lake and Black Lake. Within a few feet of this fork keep left toward The Loch. (The right fork continues to Lake Haiyaha.) In 0.8 mile farther, you reach The Loch. This peaceful and lovely lake is well worth a prolonged visit. Continue then by trail along the right side of the lake. From your

The Loch.

PHOTO BY BERNARD HOHMAN

arrival at The Loch it is 1.25 miles to a creek crossing and another signed fork. You go left (south). (The right fork ascends more steeply to Andrews Tarn and Glacier.) The trail now brings you into a beautiful high valley with Timberline Falls prominently above. The trail steepens and passes to the right of the falls. Some careful, easy handwork is needed just before you reach the top of a rocky bench and the Lake of Glass. (On the day I was there, I was impressed with the many jumping and surfacing fish in the lake.) After some respite and awe at this gem of a lake, continue on a rough but adequate trail, initially marked by cairns, along the right side of the lake. It is 0.5 mile to trail's end at Sky Pond. The valley walls above the lake steeply rise to a ridge containing several impressive pinnacles. The route back should be a lovely jaunt. Just be sure to take the correct turns at trail intersections. Fortunately, they are well marked by signs.

SEE MAP PAGE 61

25. Saint Mary's Lake

ROUND-TRIP DISTANCE	1.4 miles
HIKING TIME	Up in 20 minutes, down in 15 minutes
STARTING ELEVATION	10,360 feet
HIGHEST ELEVATION	10,690 feet
ELEVATION GAIN	370 feet (includes 20 extra feet each way)
DIFFICULTY	Easy
MAPS	Trails Illustrated, Winter Park/Central City/Rollins Pass, Number 103 Empire 7.5 minute Clear Creek County Arapaho National Forest

COMMENT: Saint Mary's Lake lies in a steep bowl just below the Saint Mary's Glacier. Located less than 50 miles west of Central Denver, this short hike is scenic, relatively easy, and ideal for families. The route follows a rough, rocky road and should be passable from the second half of May into late November. Saint Marys Glacier is really a permanent snowfield and not a glacier.

GETTING THERE: From Interstate 70, just west of Idaho Springs, take exit 238 and drive north on Fall River Road for 9.0 miles and park in the open area on the right, opposite the trailhead. (If this lot is full, there is a larger area on the west side of the road 0.1 mile back down the road.)

THE HIKE: Start walking north up the road at a sign. As you ascend the wide road, which enters the forest, take two successive left forks and stay on the main, ascending road. The road becomes a trail shortly before the lovely lake. The extensive Saint Mary's Glacier lies above to the north-northwest. Enjoy the beauty before returning on your ascent route.

Saint Mary's Lake.   PHOTO BY JOE LEAHY

Saint Mary's Lake.

PHOTO BY RICH WEBB

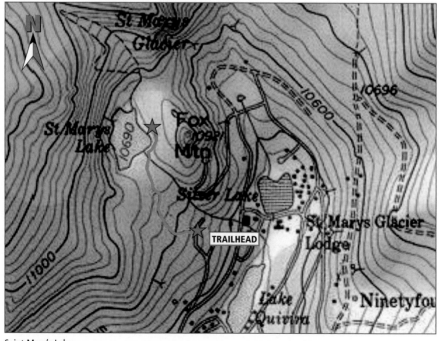

Saint Mary's Lake.

26. Chinns Lake, Sherwin Lake, and Slater Lake

ROUND-TRIP DISTANCE	4 miles
HIKING TIME	Up in 68 minutes, down in 55 minutes
STARTING ELEVATION	10,400 feet
HIGHEST ELEVATION	11,395 feet
ELEVATION GAIN	1,045 feet (includes 50 extra feet)
DIFFICULTY	Easy
MAPS	Trails Illustrated, Winter Park/Central City/Rollins Pass, Number 103 Empire 7.5 minute Clear Creek County Arapaho National Forest

COMMENT: This easy hike to three lakes is less than 50 miles from central Denver. Gentle, grassy slopes of the Continental Divide highlight this outing and invite the hiker to proceed above Slater Lake, the highest of the three lakes. Witter Peak and Mount Eva hover overhead.

GETTING THERE: From west of Idaho Springs on Interstate 70, take exit 238 and drive north on the Fall River Road for 6.8 miles. Then take the unpaved road on the left as Fall River Road turns sharply to the right. Follow this rough, main, dirt road up the valley for 2.4 miles and park off road at a fork. Two metal poles flank the road straight ahead. Most regular cars can reach this point.

THE HIKE: Start walking up the left fork of the road to the west-southwest. Follow the main road as it rises steeply to a fork just before Chinns Lake. Go left around an abandoned cabin at Chinns Lake and continue a few hundred yards to the dam at Sherwin Lake. Witter Peak is the imposing mountain to the southwest. Continue north across the dam and follow the road as it rises steeply to the right and then switches back and up into the trees. Within 100 feet after entering the forest, the main trail begins to descend. Go left here (west-northwest) on a footpath. Follow this faint trail generally up to the northwest to reach lovely, isolated Slater Lake. If you lose the trail below the lake, head toward Mount Eva to the west-northwest, find the creek emanating from Slater Lake and follow it to the lake. On your return, remember how you ascended from the dam at Sherwin Lake.

Slater Lake.

PHOTO BY SANDRA PORTNER

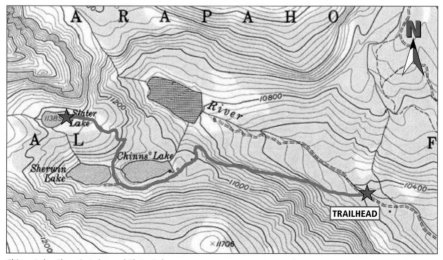

Chinns Lake, Sherwin Lake, and Slater Lake.

27. Lower and Upper Chicago Lakes

ROUND-TRIP DISTANCE	4.2 miles to lower lake and 4.8 miles to upper lake, total round-trip 9.6 miles
HIKING TIME	Up in 125 minutes, down in 130 minutes
STARTING ELEVATION	10,680 feet
HIGHEST ELEVATION	11,740 feet (Upper Chicago Lake)
ELEVATION GAIN	2,260 feet (includes 600 extra feet each way)
DIFFICULTY	Moderate
MAPS	Trails Illustrated, Idaho Springs/Georgetown/ Loveland Pass, Number 104 Idaho Springs 7.5 minute Mount Evans 7.5 minute Clear Creek County Arapaho National Forest

COMMENT: The peaceful Chicago Lakes are encased on three sides by a sheer, rocky bowl with high peaks looming above. The lower lake has more vegetation and the upper lake is more alpine. This route begins near Echo Lake and winds down into a valley and crosses Chicago Creek before joining the road, which ends just above Chicago Creek Reservoir. From road end a good trail then leads to both of these high lakes.

GETTING THERE: From Idaho Springs, drive south from Interstate 70 (exit 240) on Colorado 103 for 13.1 miles and turn right onto Colorado 5. Park on the left, either just before the barrier at the beginning of Colorado 5 (the Mount Evans Road) or just beyond it on the left, if it is open. This point can also be reached by driving 18 miles from Colorado 74 at Bergen Park, on Colorado 103.

THE HIKE: Start hiking south-southwest on Trail 52 from the sign just off of Colorado 5, about 75 feet above the road barrier. Continue through the woods on a faint trail, which is marked by blazes on the trees, and an occasional sign. After 0.5 mile, you reach a three-way trail intersection and a sign about 50 yards from the southern edge of Echo Lake. Continue westsouthwest and soon reach a ledge trail with the valley below to your right. Descend by switchbacks and finally cross Chicago Creek on a few logs and quickly reach a T at a road. Go left and ascend 0.4 mile to the Chicago Creek Reservoir. The road passes to the right and ends in 100 yards, just past two cabins. At a Mount Evans Wilderness Area sign a clear trail enters the trees

Upper Chicago Lake.

PHOTO BY DAVID THOMAS

and continues up the valley, with Chicago Creek down on your left. It is 0.8 mile from road end to a side creek crossing and 0.4 mile further to Lower Chicago Lake. A left fork descends to the lower lake and the right fork trail winds around and above the lower lake, through some rocks, to gain the more barren upper lake in 0.6 mile further. Return as you ascended.

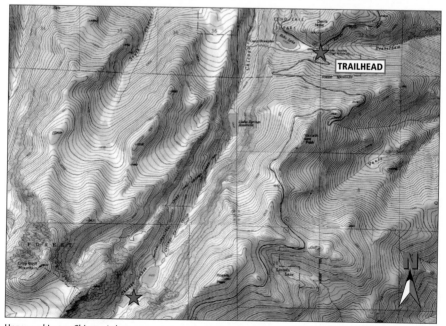

Upper and Lower Chicago Lakes.

28. Abyss Lake

ROUND-TRIP DISTANCE	7.2 miles
HIKING TIME	Out in 119 minutes, back in 118 minutes
STARTING ELEVATION	13,300 feet
HIGHEST ELEVATION	13,523 feet (Epaulet Mountain)
ELEVATION GAIN	2,346 feet (includes 2,123 extra feet)
DIFFICULTY	Moderate
MAPS	Trails Illustrated, Idaho Springs/Georgetown/ Loveland Pass, Number 104 Mount Evans 7.5 minute Clear Creek County Arapaho National Forest

COMMENT: Abyss Lake is tucked into a rocky bowl between two Fourteeners: Mount Evans and Mount Bierstadt. The most frequently used route begins from Geneva Park on the south side of the Guanella Pass Road and extends 8 miles to reach this very high lake. This other, easier, route begins considerably above timberline from the Mount Evans Road, crosses Epaulet Mountain and then descends south in a clockwise direction, then west and finally northwest into the drainage from Abyss Lake. A trail is then reached which ascends northwest to the lake. There is considerable elevation gain on the return to your high trailhead. This route avoids the dangerous, steep rocks on the western flanks of Mount Evans and Epaulet Mountain.

GETTING THERE: From the intersection of Colorado 103 and Colorado 5 (the Mount Evans Road) near Echo Lake, drive 11.3 miles on the paved Colorado 5 to the most southern switchback to the right. Park off the road at this curve. A fee is required on the Mount Evans Road.

THE HIKE: Begin your hike south-southeast toward the rocky high point. Lose some elevation before crossing over the top of Epaulet Mountain at 13,523 feet. Abyss Lake will be visible to the northwest. Descend south about 0.6 mile over boulders and tundra and gradually curve in a clockwise direction. Then descend to the northwest a grassy slope with occasional rocks. Follow this slope down into the valley and generally persist in a northwesterly direction to finally reach the trail, which has just crossed the Lake Fork of Scott Gomer Creek. Then stay on the trail 1.5 miles up and northwest to austere Abyss Lake, surrounded by rocks. The formation called "The

Abyss Lake.

PHOTO BY CLIF REED

Sawtooth" looms above to the northwest. Mount Bierstadt lies to the south and Mount Evans to the north-northeast. I advise that you retrace your route back to your vehicle and avoid any attempts at a short cut. The return route is the more difficult half of this hike.

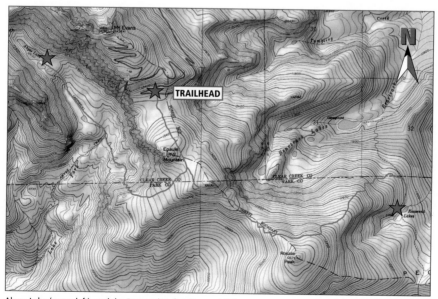

Abyss Lake (upper left), and the Roosevelt Lakes (lower right).

29. The Roosevelt Lakes

ROUND-TRIP DISTANCE	8.8 miles
HIKING TIME	Down in 125 minutes, back up to trailhead in 148 minutes
STARTING ELEVATION	13,280 feet
HIGHEST ELEVATION	13,400 feet
LOWEST ELEVATION	11,742 feet
ELEVATION GAIN	2,268 feet (includes 2,148 extra feet)
DIFFICULTY	Moderate
MAPS	Trails Illustrated, Idaho Springs/Georgetown/ Loveland Pass, Number 104 Mount Evans 7.5 minute Harris Park 7.5 minute Clear Creek County Arapaho National Forest

COMMENT: The Roosevelt Lakes can be reached several ways on foot. This is the easiest route and is all above treeline and without trail in the vast Mount Evans Wilderness. Starting from above and ending below at timberline, this is a different type of outing, one that will require a compass and some route finding. You may encounter Rocky Mountain goats, which abound in this wilderness.

GETTING THERE: Drive to Echo Lake on Colorado 103 south of Idaho Springs. Set your mileage to zero and begin up the Mount Evans Road (Colorado 5). Pay an entry fee and follow the paved road up above timberline. Pass Summit Lake on the right at mile 8.9. After 2 more miles, park on the left, about 200 yards before a sharp road turn to the right.

THE HIKE: Start hiking to the southeast and lose a little elevation before passing along the left side of Epaulet Mountain. Stay west (right) of two steep couloirs leading down to the Beartrack Lakes on the left. Then angle eastward over tundra and rock and angle around to the left of Rosalie Peak's shoulder. Soon the two Roosevelt Lakes come into view below and a trail running north and south. The Pegmatite Points lie to the east-southeast and the trail leading over the ridge to Deer Creek can be seen to the south-southeast. Reverse your compass readings for the trailless return back to your vehicle on the Mount Evans Road.

One of the Roosevelt Lakes.

PHOTO BY DAVE MULLER

SEE MAP PAGE 71

30. Lower and Upper Square Top Lakes

ROUND-TRIP DISTANCE	4.8 miles
HIKING TIME	Up in 65 minutes, down in 60 minutes
STARTING ELEVATION	11,669 feet (Guanella Pass)
HIGHEST ELEVATION	12,288 feet
ELEVATION GAIN	891 feet (includes 136 extra feet each way)
DIFFICULTY	Moderate
MAPS	Trails Illustrated, Idaho Springs/Georgetown/ Loveland Pass, Number 104 Mount Evans 7.5 minute Clear Creek County Pike National Forest

COMMENT: Here is a hike above timberline with great vistas and located less than 55 miles from central Denver. The short length and modest elevation gain to both Square Top lakes make it ideal for young and old and helps to promote adjustment to the higher elevations. The trail should be passable from June until mid-October. The Guanella Pass Road is open most of the year.

GETTING THERE: From either Georgetown on the north or Grant to the south drive to Guanella Pass and park in the open area on the east side of the pass. Regular cars can reach Guanella Pass.

THE HIKE: Start across the road on the trail to the west. Within 300 yards keep straight and lose some elevation as this old road falls and rises to the west and southwest. Keep left at two forks and generally head for the foot of Square Top Mountain. A few small creeks are traversed as the trail leads to the eastern edge of the lower of the two Square Top Lakes. To reach the upper lake, pass around to the left of the lower lake and avoid the willows. Use the road for another 0.4 mile before angling northwest to cross its outflow and reach Upper Square Top Lake. Square Top Mountain hovers above to the west-southwest. Mount Evans is east-northeast. Mount Bierstadt lies due east and Geneva Mountain and Mount Logan to the southeast. Return as you came, back to Guanella Pass.

Lower Square Top Lake.   PHOTO BY DAVE MULLER

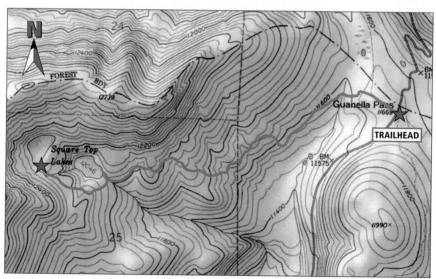

Lower and Upper Square Top Lakes.

31. Pumphouse Lake and Corona Lake

ROUND-TRIP DISTANCE	2 miles
HIKING TIME	Out in 25 minutes, back in 21 minutes
STARTING ELEVATION	11,600 feet
HIGHEST ELEVATION	11,600 feet
ELEVATION GAIN	544 feet (includes an extra 75 feet each way)
DIFFICULTY	Easy
MAPS	Trails Illustrated, Winter Park/Central City/Rollins Pass, Number 103 East Portal 7.5 minute Grand County Number 4 Arapaho National Forest

COMMENT: The Rollins Pass Road from U.S. 40 allows easy access to some beautiful high country. Grassy slopes lie below the Continental Divide and there are many lakes and trails. This easy hike to Pumphouse and Corona Lakes descends from the Rollins Pass Road to smaller Pumphouse Lake, below Mount Epworth, and then continues over to more isolated and prettier Corona Lake, which is named after a former settlement around Rollins Pass.

GETTING THERE: From U.S. 40 at Berthoud Pass, drive north for 11.5 miles and, before reaching the town of Winter Park, turn right onto the Rollins Pass Road and set your mileage to zero. Drive up this excellent, unpaved road for 12.9 miles and park off road at the unmarked trailhead. En route to

Pumphouse Lake.   PHOTO BY SANDRA PORTNER

this point, keep straight at mile 3.7 on Road 149 and continue straight again at mile 6.4.

THE HIKE: Begin on foot down to the north-northwest on an old, rough road. Within 100 yards, take the trail on your left (north) and leave the rough road. After 0.3 mile, you pass Pumphouse Lake, lying 50 yards down to the left. Two side trails descend to the lake. Past Pumphouse Lake, continue generally north-northwest, cross the outflow from Pumphouse Lake and quickly reach a split in the trail. Take the right fork and descend north to another crossing of the outflow creek. (The left fork descends west along Ranch Creek.) The trail then meanders across beautiful terrain to reach an overlook of Corona Lake before descending to its banks beneath the Continental Divide to the north. The return provides most of this hike's elevation gain.

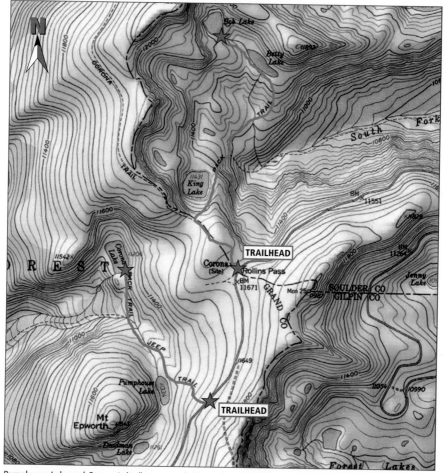

Pumphouse Lake and Corona Lake (lower route). King Lake, Betty Lake, and Bob Lake (upper route).

32. King Lake, Betty Lake, and Bob Lake

ROUND-TRIP DISTANCE	4.2 miles
HIKING TIME	Out in 64 minutes, back in 64 minutes
STARTING ELEVATION	11,660 feet
HIGHEST ELEVATION	11,690 feet
ELEVATION GAIN	980 feet (includes 950 extra feet)
DIFFICULTY	Moderate
MAPS	Trails Illustrated, Winter Park/Central City/Rollins Pass, Number 103 East Portal 7.5 minute Boulder County Roosevelt National Forest

COMMENT: The hike from Rollins Pass to King, Betty and Bob Lakes is gentle enough for hikers of all ages. The vistas are great and in mid-July, especially, the flowers can be extraordinary. The area is also full of history, as a railroad ran over Rollins Pass until 1928 and the town of Corona was located here. This route begins high on the Continental Divide, passes King Lake, drops to a creek crossing, and then rises to adjacent Betty and Bob Lakes.

GETTING THERE: On U.S. 40, drive north 11.8 miles from Berthoud Pass, or south from Vasquez Road in Winter Park for 1.7 miles. Then ascend the Rollins Pass Road (also called the Moffat Road) for 13.8 miles and park in a designated area by the sign at Rollins Pass. Stay on the main dirt road to reach this point. At a five-way intersection at mile 3.7 from U.S. 40, take the

King Lake.   PHOTO BY DOUG REESE

Betty Lake.

PHOTO BY DOUG REESE

second road on the right; at a four-way intersection at mile 6.4, keep straight, and stay left at mile 13.7. Although the road gets a bit rough toward the end, regular cars can reach Rollins Pass.

THE HIKE: Start on foot to the northwest from Rollins Pass and quickly gain the trail, which passes wilderness signs and the foundation of a building from the former town of Corona on the right. After 0.3 mile from Rollins Pass, you will reach a pole at a trail fork. King Lake will now be visible below on your right (north). Take the right fork and descend northeast past King Lake. Follow the main trail and avoid less defined side paths. Descend to a creek crossing followed by a sign at a fork. This creek is the lowest point of this outing. Go left and ascend a fainter trail northeast. Occasional cairns help you follow the trail through the bushes to reach serene Betty Lake. The trail continues along the left side of the lake, crosses its outlet, and becomes faint as it ascends to the left of the drainage to a bench. Then turn right, lose a little elevation, and cross some boulders before reaching the edge of Bob Lake (11,580 feet), nestled in an impressive rocky cirque. Enjoy the lovely setting before retracing the route back to Rollins Pass.

SEE MAP PAGE 77

33. Heart Lake and Rogers Pass Lake

ROUND-TRIP DISTANCE	2.5 miles to Rogers Pass, 0.9 mile to Heart Lake, 0.4 mile to Rogers Pass Lake (Total 3.8 miles each way)
HIKING TIME	Up to Rogers Pass in 70 minutes, down to Heart Lake in 16 minutes, over to Rogers Pass Lake in 8 minutes, back in 70 minutes (Total 164 minutes)
STARTING ELEVATION	11,160 feet
HIGHEST ELEVATION	11,870 feet
ELEVATION GAIN	1,645 feet (includes 935 extra feet)
DIFFICULTY	Moderate
MAPS	Trails Illustrated, Winter Park/Central City, Rollins Pass, Number 103 Empire 7.5 minute East Portal 7.5 minute Gilpin County Grand County Number 4 Arapaho National Forest

COMMENT: Heart Lake and Rogers Pass Lake are most readily reached from the north via the Rollins Pass Road and Rogers Pass. They can also be approached from the East Portal of the Moffat Tunnel. The season for this hike is from the middle of July through October. On the way to Rogers Pass on the Continental Divide, you are mostly above timberline and have great views, especially of the Winter Park Ski Area and of James Peak.

GETTING THERE: From Berthoud Pass, drive north on U.S. 40 for 11.5 miles and turn right onto the Rollins Pass Road (Number 149). Follow this excellent dirt road for 10.6 miles and park off road at Riflesight Notch. En route to this point, stay on the main road and keep straight at mile 3.7 and at mile 6.4. Regular cars can reach this point from July through October when the road is clear of snow.

THE HIKE: Begin to the south up a side road leading from Riflesight Notch. After 1.25 miles through the trees, you will pass timberline and the vistas really open up. Follow the main, old mining road generally south and then southeast and reach Rogers Pass at a sign 2.5 miles from the trailhead. James Peak is very impressive to the south-southeast, as is Heart Lake down to the north, and Rogers Pass Lake down to the east. Follow the road, which soon becomes a trail, down generally northeast for almost a mile to lovely Heart

Heart Lake.

PHOTO BY DAVE MULLER

Lake. Next, angle over to the southeast 0.4 mile to small Rogers Pass Lake before ascending 750 feet back to Rogers Pass and your return to Riflesight Notch.

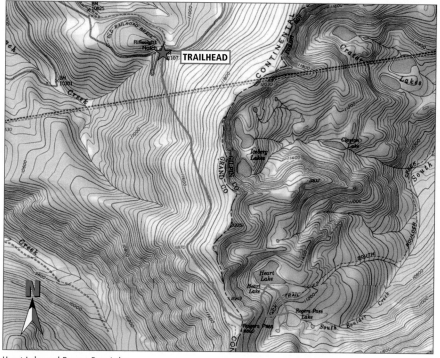

Heart Lake and Rogers Pass Lake.

34. Devils Thumb Lake

ROUND-TRIP DISTANCE	3.8 miles to Devils Thumb Pass, 1 mile further to Devils Thumb Lake (Total 4.8 miles each way) Round-trip 9.6 miles
HIKING TIME	Up to the pass in 108 minutes, down to the lake in 34 minutes (Total return time 110 minutes)
STARTING ELEVATION	9,600 feet
HIGHEST ELEVATION	11,747 feet (Devils Thumb Pass)
ELEVATION GAIN	3,074 feet (includes 927 total extra feet
DIFFICULTY	More difficult
MAPS	Trails Illustrated, Winter Park/Central City/Rollins Pass, Number 103 East Portal 7.5 minute Boulder County Grand County Number 4 Arapaho and Roosevelt National Forests

COMMENT: The trail to the Continental Divide and Devils Thumb Pass from the west uses the Continental Divide Trail and part of the Indian Peaks Wilderness. Bikes are forbidden. This was formerly called the Corona Trail.

The good trail ascends gently to a wide meadow, called Devils Thumb Park. It then ascends easterly, crosses Cabin Creek and rises more steeply to lovely, open slopes below the Continental Divide. Some switchbacks then take you past cairns and wooden poles to Devils Thumb Pass. Devils Thumb and Devils Thumb Lake are now visible. A trail then will lead you to a 600 foot descent to the picturesque lake.

GETTING THERE: From the stoplight in Fraser on U.S. 40, drive north 0.6 mile and turn right onto Grand County Road 8 and set your odometer to zero. Keep left after 0.9 mile and go left again at mile 2.5, mile 6.1, and mile 7.2. You are now on Road 128 going north. At mile 8.3, turn right onto a side road at a small sign signifying the Continental Divide Scenic Trail. Follow this road for 0.3 mile and park at road end, with an aqueduct on the right. The key intersections have been noted, but there are many side roads along this route to the trailhead. The road is bumpy at times, but regular cars can reach this parking area.

THE HIKE: From the parking area, begin north-northeast on the clear trail. Within 50 yards keep left at a sign. Stay left again at the next fork 0.6 mile farther. Another 0.1 mile brings you to a signed fork. Go right (northeast)

Devils Thumb Lake.

PHOTO BY DAVE MULLER

here. (The left fork is the former High Lonesome Trail, which is now part of the Continental Divide Trail. This segment leads to Monarch Lake.) After another 0.6 mile, cross Cabin Creek. (This is easier in mid- to late-hiking season, due to the heavy early runoff.) The trail then rises more steeply, with another creek crossing, for 1.8 more miles to enter the Indian Peaks Wilderness and to emerge into a high meadow below rocky peaks. Continue by trail up to Devils Thumb Pass on the ridge. The rocky projection, known as Devils Thumb, lies to the north-northeast and Devils Thumb Lake down to the east. Follow the ridge and cairns to the right (south) and look for the trail descending to the lake about 250 yards from the pass. Descend 1 mile to Devils Thumb Lake and enjoy the far point of this hike. Return as you ascended and be careful to stay on the trail. It's very easy to get lost in the Rocky Mountains.

Devils Thumb Lake.

35. Monarch Lake Loop

ROUND-TRIP DISTANCE	3.8 miles (total loop)
HIKING TIME	96 minutes (total loop)
STARTING ELEVATION	8,330 feet
HIGHEST ELEVATION	8,361 feet
ELEVATION GAIN	631 feet (includes 600 extra feet)
DIFFICULTY	Easy
MAPS	Trails Illustrated, Indian Peaks/Gold Hill, Number 102 Monarch Lake 7.5 minute Grand County Number 2 Arapaho National Forest

COMMENT: With picnic tables, toilets, and informational signs near the trail-head, the loop around Monarch Lake Provides an easy, refreshing family hike in the beautiful Indian Peaks Wilderness. Bikes are forbidden and dogs must be kept on a leash. The hike begins at a confluence of trails. The Cascade Creek Trail goes to the left and the Southside Trail, which is part of the Continental Divide Trail, proceeds to the right over the dam, and connects eventually with both the High Lonesome Trail and the Cascade Creek Trail.

GETTING THERE: From U.S. 40 at the western edge of Granby, drive north on U.S. 34 for 5.4 miles. Then turn right on the Arapaho Bay Road (Grand County Number 6) and drive on the good, main road for another 9.5 miles to a road barrier at Monarch Lake. Park nearby.

THE HIKE: For a clockwise loop around the lake, begin east-southeast on the left fork at the big trail sign at the lake. Follow this Cascade Creek Trail alongside the lake, pass the wilderness boundary and then enter the woods, with

Monarch Lake.   PHOTO BY DAVE MULLER

Monarch Lake.

PHOTO BY DAVE COOPER

the creek on your right, until you reach a signed fork. Go to the right (south-west) on the Southside Trail. Soon cross Buchanan Creek, and 0.6 mile further, cross Arapaho Creek, both on sturdy bridges. Within 0.25 mile further, pass the High Lonesome Trail and a cabin ruin on your left and continue straight ahead (west). Before long you leave the wilderness area and pass a large, old abandoned engine. Continue through the thin forest with Monarch Lake on your right. The trail becomes less defined here but can still be followed. Pass between two large log bins before curving around the edge of the lake to the dam, the end of the loop, and your vehicle 100 yards to the left.

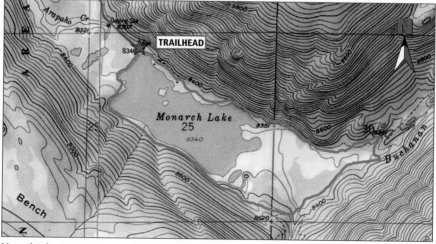

Monarch Lake.

85

36. Watanga Lake

ROUND-TRIP DISTANCE	9 miles
HIKING TIME	Up in 143 minutes, down in 105 minutes
STARTING ELEVATION	8,315 feet
HIGHEST ELEVATION	10,780 feet
ELEVATION GAIN	2,895 feet (includes 215 extra feet each way)
DIFFICULTY	More difficult
MAPS	Trails Illustrated, Indian Peaks, Number 102 or Rocky Mountain National Park, Number 200 Shadow Mountain 7.5 minute Isolation Peak 7.5 minute Grand County Number 2 Arapaho National Forest

COMMENT: Watanga (Black Coyote) was a Southern Arapaho Chief in the late 1800's. The lake destination of this hike, the creek leading from it, and the mountain to its east, are all named in his honor. The route to Watanga Lake lies in a more remote part of the Indian Peaks Wilderness north of Lake Granby. The trail rises steeply alongside the Roaring Fork for almost 3 miles and then ascends over a rougher trail along Watanga Creek to the isolated, lovely lake at 10,780 feet.

GETTING THERE: From the intersection with U.S. 40 west of Granby, drive north on U.S. 34 for 5.4 miles and turn right onto Forest Road 125. Follow this good, dirt road around the southeastern edge of Lake Granby for a total of 9.7 miles and park at the Roaring Fork Trailhead. En route to this point, go left at mile 1.2, right at mile 1.4, left at mile 8.8, and drive through the campground.

THE HIKE: Start north on foot from the parking area on the Roaring Fork Trail. After a few hundred level yards, take the right fork past a sign board and trail register and ascend some switchbacks steeply to the north, with the Roaring Fork to your left (west). After 1.3 miles from the parking area, cross the Roaring Fork on two logs and continue up the valley for another 1.5 miles to a right trail fork and another creek crossing. After crossing the creek, keep left at a T and within 100 yards arrive at a trail sign at a fork in the trail. The Roaring Fork Trail continues up to the right. You follow the left fork north-northeast to Watanga Lake. The trail becomes rougher and

Watanga Lake.

PHOTO BY MARIA SMITH

less maintained from this point onward. After 0.25 mile from the last fork, the trail arrives at another creek crossing, but there is no log or bridge to assist you. Wade across the creek and regain the trail as it continues to the right along the creek. (This is the reason that the late season is best for this hike.) Or, you can avoid the creek crossing and bushwhack to your right several hundred yards, cross two smaller creeks, and rejoin the trail just after a log crosses the creek. Ascend the valley on the trail, cross Watanga Creek twice, pass over some fallen logs that block the trail and, after some switchbacks, arrive at a ridge. Then descend slightly to beautiful Watanga Lake. Faint trails continue left and right for brief segments around the lake. If you want to hike to the top of Watanga Mountain, it is 2 more easy miles east and then northeast over mostly tundra from the right fork at the lake.

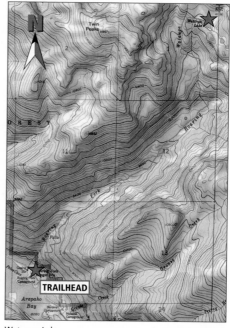

Watanga Lake.

37. Shadow Mountain Lake and Columbine Bay

ROUND-TRIP DISTANCE	9.2 miles
HIKING TIME	Out in 103 minutes, back in 93 minutes
STARTING ELEVATION	8,400 feet
HIGHEST ELEVATION	8,485 feet
LOWEST ELEVATION	8,286 feet
ELEVATION GAIN	617 feet (includes 333 extra feet)
DIFFICULTY	Moderate
MAPS	Trails Illustrated, Rocky Mountain National Park, Number 200 Shadow Mountain 7.5 minute Grand County Number 2

COMMENT: This outing on the southwestern edge of beautiful Rocky Mountain National Park features lots of lakeside hiking and little elevation gain. At present, no entrance fee is required and the trails and signs are excellent. Pets and bicycles are prohibited on these national park trails.

GETTING THERE: From U.S. 40, west of Granby, drive north on U.S. 34 for 14.3 miles and turn right into Grand Lake Village. Set your mileage at zero. After 0.2 mile, turn right onto Elk Avenue. Two tenths of a mile farther turn left on Marina Drive. After one block, turn right on Lakeside. Drive for another 0.2 mile before turning right on Jericho Road and crossing a bridge. It is another half mile to the east shore trailhead on the left.

THE HIKE: From the parking area, take the East Shore Trail to the southeast, curve right, and enter Rocky Mountain National Park after 0.5 mile. With Shadow Mountain Lake on the right, walk another mile and take the right fork (south) and stay on the Continental Divide Trail. (The trail on the left ascends to the Shadow Mountain Lookout.) Within another 50 yards, you reach a key fork. Continue on the left trail, which is still the Continental Divide Trail, and you will later return by way of the trail on the right. Continue through the sparse forest and soon traverse vast open fields before reaching a signed fork. The trail to the right leads to the Shadow Mountain Dam, but you continue straight another 1.4 miles to Columbine Creek. Keep left at two further intersections and hike alongside the Colorado River, which connects Shadow Mountain Lake with Lake Granby. At Columbine

Shadow Mountain Lake from the dam.

PHOTO BY JEFF MILLER

Creek, there is a bridge that is the terminus of this hike. (The East Shore Trail continues southeast.) Columbine Creek empties into Columbine Bay, a popular fishing area. On your return, you can retrace your route or you can make a loop by taking the first left fork at a pole and staying close to the Colorado River. This trail takes you to the right side of Shadow Mountain Dam and then along the right side of Shadow Mountain Lake, until you reach a junction with your outgoing route. Go left at this intersection and return to the trailhead.

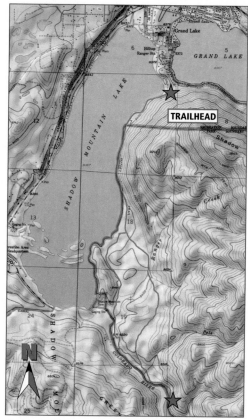

Shadow Mountain Lake.

89

38. Lone Pine Lake, Lake Verna, Spirit Lake, and Fourth Lake

ROUND-TRIP DISTANCE	16 miles (5.5 miles to Lone Pine Lake, 1.4 more miles to Lake Verna, 0.6 mile further to Spirit Lake and 0.5 mile further to Fourth Lake)
HIKING TIME	Up in 210 minutes, down in 195 minutes
STARTING ELEVATION	8,390 feet
HIGHEST ELEVATION	10,390 feet
ELEVATION GAIN	5,070 feet (includes 1,535 extra feet each way)
DIFFICULTY	Most difficult
MAPS	Trails Illustrated, Rocky Mountain National Park, Number 200 Isolation Peak 7.5 minute Shadow Mountain 7.5 minute Grand County Number 2

COMMENT: The East Inlet Trail, at the edge of Grand Lake, is not heavily used, even though it is a part of Rocky Mountain National Park. No fee is required and pets are excluded. This long trail traverses a lengthy, lovely meadow before ascending to a series of majestic lakes and ending below some very impressive, rugged peaks. The rushing water of the East Inlet is encountered throughout the trail and several campsites are available along the route.

GETTING THERE: From U.S. 40 at the western edge of Granby, drive north on U.S. 34 for 14.4 miles and turn right into the town of Grand Lake. After 0.3 mile, take a left fork and drive 2.1 miles further to the parking area at the East Inlet Trailhead of Rocky Mountain National Park. This parking area lies at the end of the road at the eastern end of Grand Lake.

THE HIKE: Begin hiking to the southeast past a signboard and follow the good trail up the valley. After 0.3 mile, pass a short side-trail on the right to an overview of the roaring waters of Adams Falls. Continue straight past this side-trail along the left side of a large meadow, past a series of designated campsites and cascading waters, up to the serenity of Lone Pine Lake, after 5.5 miles from the trailhead. A single tree on a small rocky island at the south end of the lake gives it its name. Continue by trail to the right of the lake and ascend along scenic cliffs another 1.4 miles to large Lake Verna on the right. (Before reaching this lake, there are some ponds and pools that are

Lone Pine Lake.

PHOTO BY JEFF MILLER

not to be confused with the grandeur of Lake Verna.) Beyond the middle of Lake Verna, an unimproved trail continues along the left side of the lake, past its sandy shores another 0.6 mile to smaller yet magnificent Spirit Lake, with rocky cliffs above its southern edge. The trail becomes even fainter and more difficult to follow as it proceeds easterly for the last 0.5 mile to Fourth Lake. If you lose the trail, just follow the creek. The peaks above and beyond this lake are memorable. Isolation Peak lies to the south-southeast. Mount Alice is northeast and Tanima Peak looms to the east. There is Fifth Lake, about 1 mile further up the valley to the southeast, for the especially hardy hiker. Refuel your rockets before your long but lovely return back down into the East Inlet Valley and the trailhead.

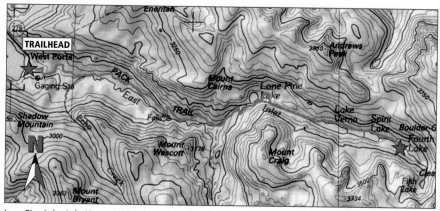

Lone Pine Lake, Lake Verna, Spirit Lake, and Fourth Lake.

39. Bowen Lake

ROUND-TRIP DISTANCE	16.2 miles
HIKING TIME	Up in 240 minutes, down in 209 minutes
STARTING ELEVATION	8,810 feet
HIGHEST ELEVATION	11,029 feet
ELEVATION GAIN	3,159 feet (includes 470 extra feet each way)
DIFFICULTY	Most difficult
MAPS	Trails Illustrated, Rocky Mountain National Park, Number 200 Grand Lake 7.5 minute Bowen Mountain 7.5 minute Grand County Number 2 Arapaho National Forest

COMMENT: The long trek to Bowen Lake begins in Rocky Mountain National Park and continues into the Never Summer Wilderness in the Arapaho National Forest. There are several creek crossings as the trail steepens in its second half. At Bowen Lake the trail continues, to join the Wolverine Trail. Bowen Lake, Pass, and Mountain are named after James H. Bourn, a prospector who filed the Wolverine Mine claim in Colorado's early years. The name was erroneously changed over the years.

GETTING THERE: Drive on U.S. 34 from the western edge of Granby to the Grand Lake entrance of Rocky Mountain National Park. Avoid the town of Grand Lake and stay on U.S. 34 to the fee and entry station. Continue north into the park on U.S. 34 for 6.3 miles from the fee station and park on the left at the Bowen-Baker trailhead.

THE HIKE: From the parking area, go west across the Colorado River and the lovely Kawuneeche Valley. As you enter the forest, take the left (southwest) fork, as the path on the right leads to Baker Gulch. Continue past a road barrier, over a stone bridge, and past a building and picnic tables before crossing a creek on the right and following the clear trail up to the Never Summer Wilderness boundary and a register. You have hiked 0.7 mile and are now leaving Rocky Mountain National Park. After another 0.3 mile, keep left at an unmarked trail intersection. Follow the gradual trail through the trees for another 1.3 miles and reach a T. Go right (west-southwest) as the route becomes steeper. There will be two significant creek crossings and perhaps

Bowen Lake.

some fallen trees on the trail as you rise to the Blue Lake Trail on the right, at mile 5.6 of this trek. Ascend to the west as the scenery opens up. Soon cross a ridge and descend to another creek crossing before reaching the intersection with the Bowen Lake Trail on the left at a small sign. Leave the Bowen Gulch Trail and go south another 1.7 miles with three creek crossings before arriving at lovely Bowen Lake with Cascade Mountain towering above to the west. The trail continues along the left side of the lake. Rest, replenish, and enjoy the beauty before the lengthy return to the Bowen-Baker Trailhead.

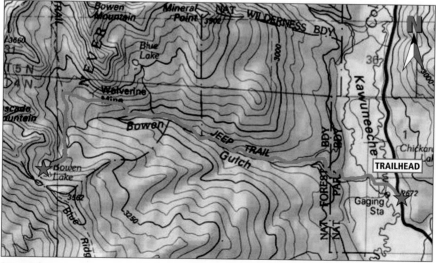

Bowen Lake.

40. Haynach Lake

ROUND-TRIP DISTANCE	16.4 miles
HIKING TIME	Up in 234 minutes, down in 188 minutes
STARTING ELEVATION	8,790 feet
HIGHEST ELEVATION	11,103 feet
ELEVATION GAIN	3,898 feet (includes 1,585 extra feet)
DIFFICULTY	Most difficult
MAPS	Trails Illustrated, Rocky Mountain National Park, Number 200 Grand Lake 7.5 minute Grand County Number 2

COMMENT: The long route to Haynach Lake in the western part of Rocky Mountain National Park follows the Tonahutu Creek Trail, which is also part of the Continental Divide Trail. The well-marked trail passes Big Meadows, Granite Falls, and several campgrounds before reaching a very scenic lake at the foot of Nakai Peak. Haynach is an Arapaho word meaning "snow water." Snow tends to remain in the upper areas of this hike well into June. I would recommend you wait until July to try it. Since this lake is so distant, relatively few people visit it. Rocky Mountain National Park rules forbid bicycles, weapons, or pets on the trail.

GETTING THERE: From the Grand Lake entrance station, drive north on U.S. 34 into Rocky Mountain National Park for 2.5 miles and park on the right at the Green Mountain Trailhead.

THE HIKE: The trek begins by trail to the northeast from the Green Mountain Trailhead. Ascend through the forest to a ridge and then descend to a signed fork at mile 1.8. Keep left and walk north along Big Meadows, a lovely open area beneath Mount Patterson to the east. Pass by two cabin ruins. 0.5 mile from the last fork, go right (north) as the trail splits again at another sign. Follow the trail through the trees as it passes the Sunset Campground on the left and later the Sunrise Campground, also on the left. At mile 5.2, beautiful Granite Falls appears on the right, with more adjacent campgrounds. Rise to a crossing of a meadow on the left, with rocky cliffs above. Soon pass through Tonahutu Meadows. Pass more campgrounds, cross the outflow from Haynach Lake and round the corner to a key fork at mile 7.0. Here you leave the main trail and ascend left (west) toward Haynach Campground.

Haynach Lake.

PHOTO BY MARIA SMITH

The trail is steep and faint in spots as it ascends into some lovely meadows. Pass some pools on the left before the trail ends at Haynach Lake, with Nakai Peak above to the west-southwest. Relax and refresh before the lengthy return trip.

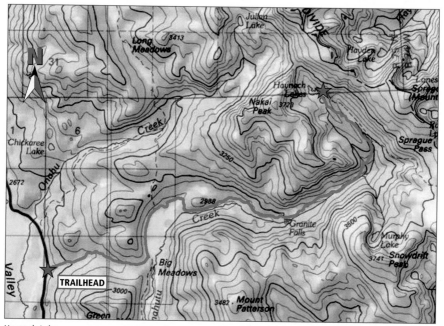

Haynach Lake.

41. Lake of the Clouds

ROUND-TRIP DISTANCE	13.2 miles
HIKING TIME	Up in 210 minutes, down in 180 minutes
STARTING ELEVATION	9,070 feet
HIGHEST ELEVATION	11,430 feet
ELEVATION GAIN	3,170 feet (includes 405 extra feet each way)
DIFFICULTY	More difficult
MAPS	Trails Illustrated, Rocky Mountain National Park, Number 200 Fall River Road 7.5 minute Mount Richthofen 7.5 minute Grand County Number 2

COMMENT: Lake of the Clouds lies in a remote northwest section of Rocky Mountain National Park. Flanked on three sides by the Never Summer Mountains and the Continental Divide, the large lake lies in an inviting rocky bowl. The route to the lake from the Colorado River trailhead is long, and without a clear trail for the final 0.75 mile and 650 feet of elevation gain.

GETTING THERE: From the Grand Lake entrance of Rocky Mountain National Park, drive north on U.S. 34 from the fee station for 9.3 miles and turn left toward the Colorado River trailhead and park in the large lot.

THE HIKE: Your hike begins on the good trail to the north-northwest. Pets and bicycles are forbidden. After 0.5 mile, go left (west) at a signed fork, cross the Colorado River and begin your uphill trek. Soon cross Opposition Creek on a small bridge and continue up through the forest to reach the road, which parallels the Grand Ditch, an irrigation canal, at mile 3.3 of the hike. Then, go to the right (north) and follow the wide road (which is blocked to public vehicular traffic) for 1.4 miles to Hitchens Gulch and a sign at a crossing of the Grand Ditch. Ascend more steeply into the trees to the south. At mile 5.5, pass the Hitchens Gulch campground on the left. The Dutchtown campground will also be on your left, at mile 5.7. Continue up another 0.1 mile to a sign pointing toward the Lake of the Clouds and stating that this is the end of the maintained trail. Here you have two good choices: either follow the primitive trail up to a vast boulder field and then follow cairns around to the left and up to the lake paralleling its outflow, or proceed directly south-southwest and pick your way up steep tundra and some rocks

Lake of the Clouds.

PHOTO BY ULLI LIMPITLAW

to the majestic Lake of the Clouds with Howard Mountain to the southwest. Lead Mountain and Mount Richthofen can be seen across the basin to the north-northwest from the edge of the lake. Enjoy the beauty and gather your strength for the long return trip to the trailhead.

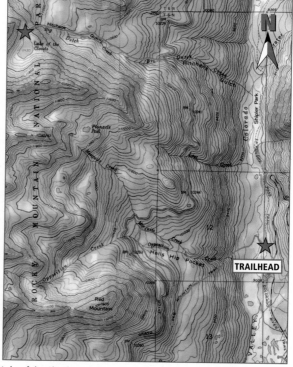

Lake of the Clouds.

42. Lost Lake (Grand County)

ROUND-TRIP DISTANCE	1.6 miles
HIKING TIME	Up in 20 minutes, down in 20 minutes
STARTING ELEVATION	9,460 feet
HIGHEST ELEVATION	9,670 feet
ELEVATION GAIN	370 feet (includes an extra 80 feet each way)
DIFFICULTY	Easy
MAPS	Trails Illustrated, Rocky Mountain National Park, Number 200 Bowen Mountain 7.5 minute Grand County Number 2 Arapaho National Forest

COMMENT: Colorado and the West are full of "Lost Lakes." This one would make a good outing for the whole family, with a picnic by the lake. The trail connects with the Wolverine Trail, which offers more strenuous possibilities.

GETTING THERE: From its intersection with U.S. 40 just west of Granby, drive north on Colorado 125 for 14.1 miles and turn right on the good dirt road to Stillwater Pass. Follow the main road for 5.7 miles and then take the left fork at a sign. Continue for 0.7 mile further to road end and park in a designated area on the right. (En route to this point from Colorado 125, keep straight at mile 1.6, right at mile 3.5, and straight at mile 4.5.) Regular cars can reach this trailhead.

Jackie Muller at Lost Lake.   PHOTO BY DAVE MULLER

Lost Lake.

PHOTO BY RICH WEBB

THE HIKE: Begin east from the parking area. Follow the blocked road as it curves south and reaches a fork after several hundred yards from the trailhead. Take the right fork. (The left route is the Wolverine Trail.) Descend into lovely forest and soon cross Willow Creek before ascending to Lost Lake. A primitive trail continues a few hundred yards along the lakeside. Gravel Mountain can be seen to the southwest and the Porphyry Peaks to the southeast. Retrace your route back to the trailhead for the return.

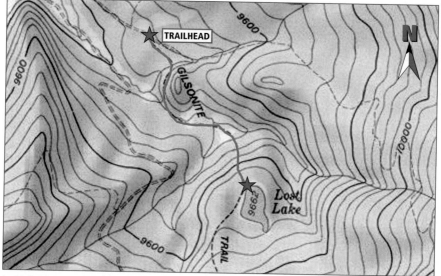

Lost Lake.

43. Lake Dinosaur

ROUND-TRIP DISTANCE	1.2 miles
HIKING TIME	Up in 15 minutes, down in 15 minutes
STARTING ELEVATION	10,087 feet
HIGHEST ELEVATION	10,248 feet
ELEVATION GAIN	227 feet (includes 66 extra feet)
DIFFICULTY	Easy
MAPS	Trails Illustrated, Clark/Buffalo Pass, Number 117 Buffalo Pass 7.5 minute Routt County Number 4 Routt National Forest

COMMENT: Lake Dinosaur, south of Buffalo Pass, is a seldom visited but lovely body of water whose shape from above suggests a dinosaur. Buffalo Pass lies on the Continental Divide just south of the Mount Zirkel Wilderness. It was the main route into Steamboat Springs from the east before the road was built over Rabbit Ears Pass.

GETTING THERE: Drive to Buffalo Pass, northeast of the town of Steamboat Springs, on Forest Road 60. From U.S. 40 in Steamboat Springs, drive north on Seventh Avenue. After 0.4 mile, turn right onto Missouri Avenue. Follow the signs to Buffalo Pass and reach an intersection with Routt County Road 36 at mile 1.6 from U.S. 40. Go left on Routt 36 for 0.8 mile and turn right onto Routt 38. Follow this main road, which becomes Forest Road 60, for 11 miles from Routt 36, and reach a four-way intersection at Buffalo Pass. (This point is 13.4 miles from U.S. 40 in Steamboat Springs.) Descend Road 310 on the right and keep straight after 0.2 mile. Continue another 3.2 miles and park along the side of the road just past a creek that passes under the road. A rocky cliff lies ahead on the right and a faint trail can be seen ascending on the right.

THE HIKE: Walk to the northwest on the sometimes-faint trail. Pass a stand of trees on the left and ascend gradually through a large, tree-lined meadow. The narrow trail at times consists of trampled grass. The route curves to the right and joins an old road. Pass a rock formation on the left before the final, gentle descent to large, serene Lake Dinosaur. Take your time at the lake since your return route will take little time.

Karen Fling O'Donnell at Lake Dinosaur.

PHOTO BY DAVE MULLER

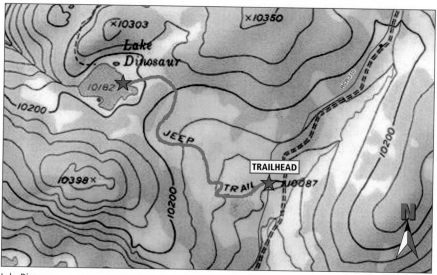

Lake Dinosaur.

44. Gold Creek Lake

ROUND-TRIP DISTANCE	6.2 miles
HIKING TIME	Up in 80 minutes, down in 68 minutes
STARTING ELEVATION	8,440 feet
HIGHEST ELEVATION	9,572 feet
ELEVATION GAIN	1,612 feet (includes 240 extra feet each way)
DIFFICULTY	Moderate
MAPS	Trails Illustrated, Hahns Peak/Steamboat Lake, Number 116 Mount Zirkel 7.5 minute Routt County Number 2 Routt National Forest

COMMENT: Located at the edge of the Routt Divide Blowdown of October 1997, the popular trail to Gold Creek Lake is especially beautiful. The rushing waters of Gold Creek parallel the trail and provide waterfalls, cascades, and a few creek crossings. As one creek crossing can be difficult, try this hike after mid-August, when the runoff is diminished.

GETTING THERE: From U.S. 40 west of Steamboat Springs, drive northwest on Routt County Road 129 for 17.6 miles. Then turn right onto the Seedhouse Road (Forest Road 400), just after passing through the town of Clark. Follow the Seedhouse Road for 11.6 miles to the end of the road at the Slavonia trailhead. En route, take the right fork at mile 8.6, go straight at mile 9.2, and left at mile 9.4. Regular cars can drive this good, dirt road to the trailhead.

Gold Creek Lake. PHOTO BY ALAN STARK

Gold Creek Lake.

PHOTO BY ALAN STARK

THE HIKE: Follow the trail from signs at the end of the parking area and enter lush forest to the north-northeast. Within 75 yards, the trail forks at a register and sign. Proceed east on the right fork. The clear trail is overgrown in places but there are many clearings and overlook areas along the way. Soon cross over a bridge and continue up the valley. 2 miles from the trailhead there is a creek crossing on a large log, followed closely by an easier crossing over rocks. The final mile to the lake uses several switchbacks and passes through an area of fallen trees, just before reaching beautiful Gold Creek Lake, with the ridge of Flattop Mountain visible to the northeast. The trail continues to several possible destinations. These include Ute Pass, Gilpin Lake, the Slavonia Work Camp, and Red Dirt Pass on the Continental Divide below Mount Zirkel. Return by your ascent trail. If you want a longer loop, return via Gilpin Lake back to the Slavonia trailhead.

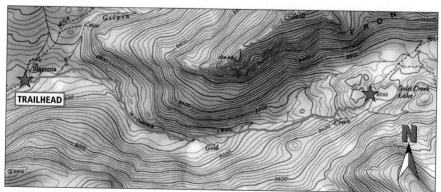

Gold Creek Lake.

103

45. Fishhook Lake, Lost Lake, and Lake Elmo

ROUND-TRIP DISTANCE	6 miles
HIKING TIME	Out in 76 minutes, back in 76 minutes
STARTING ELEVATION	10,040 feet
HIGHEST ELEVATION	10,045 feet
ELEVATION GAIN	1,045 feet (includes 1,040 extra feet)
DIFFICULTY	Moderate
MAPS	Trails Illustrated, Steamboat Springs/Rabbit Ears Pass, Number 118 Mount Werner 7.5 minute Routt County Number 4 Routt National Forest

COMMENT: This hike uses the Continental Divide Trail, which is also called the Wyoming Trail in this area. The hiker initially descends to an open valley and then gradually ascends to three beautiful lakes lying in the level meadows of the Rabbit Ears Pass area. From Lake Elmo, the highest of these three lakes, the trail continues north to several other lakes and Buffalo Pass.

GETTING THERE: From U.S. 40 on Rabbit Ears Pass, drive north on Road 315, the road to Dumont Lake. This turnoff is 6.2 miles east of West Rabbit Ears Pass and 1.4 miles west of East Rabbit Ears Pass. Follow this paved road 1.5 miles and turn left onto a dirt road at a simple Rabbit Ears Pass Monument. Drive up this road and enter the forest. Keep straight at an intersection after 0.3 mile and follow the main road for 4.0 more miles to the Base Camp trailhead. Park on the left. Although rough, this road can be negotiated by regular cars with adequate clearance.

THE HIKE: From the trailhead signs, begin to the northwest and quickly descend over 300 feet through the woods to a meadow and Fishhook Creek. With the Continental Divide always to your right, ascend to the northwest through the trees to reach Fishhook Lake at mile 1.4 from the trailhead. The curve at the northern edge of this very large lake explains it name. Continue by trail along the right side of the lake to a sign at a trail intersection. Take the right fork and, within 75 yards, reach Lost Lake at mile 1.9 from the trailhead. After visiting Lost Lake, return to the fork and climb to the right for the final 1.1 miles to a vast meadow and Lake Elmo on the left. Relax on

Fishhook Lake.

PHOTO BY DAVE MULLER

the level terrain before retracing your route. Save some energy for the final, steep ascent back to the trailhead.

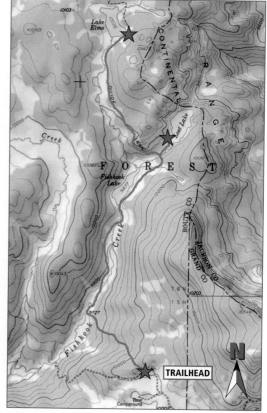

Fishhook Lake, Lost Lake, and Lake Elmo.

46. Lake Katherine

ROUND-TRIP DISTANCE	4.8 miles
HIKING TIME	Up in 68 minutes, down in 50 minutes
STARTING ELEVATION	8,915 feet
HIGHEST ELEVATION	9,884 feet
ELEVATION GAIN	1,544 feet (includes 575 extra feet)
DIFFICULTY	Moderate
MAPS	Trails Illustrated, Hahns Peak/Steamboat Lake Number 116; and Clark/Buffalo Pass/, Number 117 Mount Ethel 7.5 minute Mount Zirkel 7.5 minute Pitchpine Mountain 7.5 minute Jackson County Number 1 Routt National Forest

COMMENT: Some lakes are more striking than others. Lake Katherine ranks high in natural beauty. The teal-colored water, the green, partially timbered bowl above it, and the remnants of an old dam at its outlet, make this body of water special. Within the Mount Zirkel Wilderness and below the Continental Divide, this short hike is quite popular.

GETTING THERE: From Colorado 14 at the southern edge of Walden, drive west on Jackson County Road 12W. Keep left at mile 7.7, go right at mile 9.8, and at mile 11.9 turn left at a T onto Jackson County Road 16. Follow this good dirt road until it ends at the trailhead at mile 19.6 from Colorado 14.

Lake Katherine.   PHOTO BY DAVE MULLER

Lake Katherine.

PHOTO BY BOB WATKINS

THE HIKE: Walk west on the Lone Pine Trail (Number 1129) into the forest. Quickly pass through a fence and soon pass through a meadow before entering the wilderness area. After another smaller meadow, you reach two signed forks. Keep left at each. (The first right fork continues to the Continental Divide and the second leads to Bighorn Lake and beyond.) After continuing south on the second left fork, make a significant, unassisted creek crossing before ascending more steeply. The cascading waters from Lake Katherine will impress you as the clear trail rises to the lake. When lovely Lake Katherine comes into view, take a left fork toward its outflow. A trail on the right leads to some campsites. You may want to linger a while at this beautiful lake.

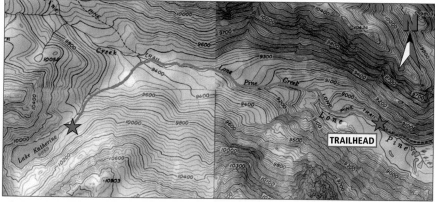

Lake Katherine.

47. Smith Lake

ROUND-TRIP DISTANCE	1.5 miles
HIKING TIME	Up in 21 minutes, down in 19 minutes
STARTING ELEVATION	10,192 feet
HIGHEST ELEVATION	10,500 feet
ELEVATION GAIN	418 feet (includes 55 extra feet each way)
DIFFICULTY	Easy
MAPS	Trails Illustrated, Flat Tops NE/Trappers Lake, Number 122 Orno Peak 7.5 minute Garfield County Number 1 Routt National Forest

COMMENT: The hike to Smith Lake is short and scenic. The foliage is lush and two ponds are encountered as you ascend into the Flat Tops Wilderness. The trail is adequate and extends around this serene lake. The lake and the creek flowing from it are named after Tom Smith, a trapper who lived in this area in the 1880s.

GETTING THERE: From Main Street in Yampa, via Colorado 131, take Garfield County Road 7 (which becomes Forest Road 900), drive 16.1 miles and park on the right at the trailhead sign. (This point is 0.6 mile before the road ends at Stillwater Reservoir.)

THE HIKE: Start walking steeply up the trail to the northwest and soon pass an unnamed pond below on your left. Avoid a side trail on the left above this pond and stay on the main trail as it rises past another pond below and on the right. Continue up and reach Smith Lake at the head of the valley. The outflow will be on your right and is easily crossed on a group of logs. A trail circles the lake and the Flat Tops can be seen above, to the west-northwest. As this hike is so short, you may wish to combine it with another in the grand Flat Tops Wilderness.

SIDEBAR: These Four Hikes

If you have three days to spend in the high country, we'd recommend the hikes to Smith, Little Causeway, Mosquito, and Hooper Lakes. Mid-week in July we found a decent campsite in the Cold Springs Campground. Did we mention that the hiking is simply superb?

Smith Lake.

PHOTO BY DAVE MULLER

SEE MAP PAGE 111

48. Little Causeway Lake

ROUND-TRIP DISTANCE	3.4 miles
HIKING TIME	Up in 45 minutes, down in 40 minutes
STARTING ELEVATION	10,275 feet
HIGHEST ELEVATION	10,760 feet
ELEVATION GAIN	695 feet (includes 210 extra feet)
DIFFICULTY	Easy
MAPS	Trails Illustrated, Flat Tops NE/Trappers Lake, Number 122 Devils Causeway 7.5 minute Orno Peak 7.5 minute Garfield County Number 1 Routt National Forest

COMMENT: Lovely Little Causeway Lake in the Flat Tops Wilderness lies at the southern foot of the Devils Causeway, a prime Colorado hiking target. The Flat Tops are honeycombed with peaks, lakes, and trails. There are several access points to this outdoor paradise.

GETTING THERE: From the south end of Main Street in Yampa, drive on Routt County Road 7, which becomes Forest Road 900, for 16.7 miles to road's end at the Stillwater Reservoir. Park in the large open area. Regular cars can easily reach this point.

THE HIKE: Start to the southwest past a signboard on the Bear River Trail. With the Stillwater Reservoir fully visible on the left, follow the trail for 0.7 mile to

Little Causeway Lake. PHOTO BY DAVE MULLER

a trail register, signboard, and fork. Ascend the right fork to the southwest. You are now on the East Fork Trail, which continues up through lovely forest and meadow for another mile to Little Causeway Lake below and on the left. A side trail descends northwest to this picturesque lake. The Devils Causeway towers above to the west-northwest. The East Fork Trail continues north to a saddle and several trails that take you deeper into the Flat Tops Wilderness.

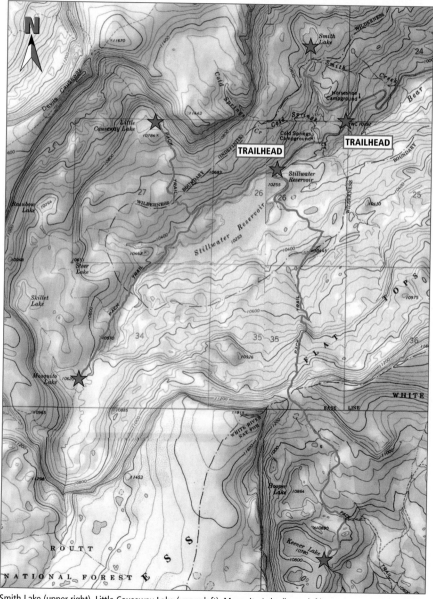

Smith Lake (upper right), Little Causeway Lake (upper left), Mosquito Lake (lower left), Hooper Lake and Keener Lake (lower right).

49. Mosquito Lake

ROUND-TRIP DISTANCE	4.4 miles
HIKING TIME	Up in 52 minutes, down in 50 minutes
STARTING ELEVATION	10,270 feet
HIGHEST ELEVATION	10,620 feet
ELEVATION GAIN	780 feet (includes 215 extra feet each way)
DIFFICULTY	Easy
MAPS	Trails Illustrated, Flat Tops NE/Trappers Lake, Number 122 Devils Causeway 7.5 minute Garfield County Number 1 Routt National Forest

COMMENT: The Flat Tops Wilderness is a huge, user-friendly area for outdoor enthusiasts in north central Colorado. The beautiful landscape is not too steep and there are many trails. Mosquito Lake is one of the shorter Flat Tops hikes, but there are many rewards. The trail overlooks large Stillwater Reservoir in its first part and makes three creek crossings before reaching the lake. Characteristic Flat Tops peaks lie above and, at the right time, the wild flowers can be splendid. I encountered only an average number of mosquitoes at the lake.

GETTING THERE: From the south end of Main Street in the town of Yampa, off of Colorado 131, drive west on Garfield Road Number 7 for 16.7 miles and park at the end of the road at Stillwater Reservoir. This road becomes Forest Road 900 en route to the trailhead parking area.

Mosquito Lake.   PHOTO BY ALAN STARK

Mosquito Lake.

PHOTO BY ALAN STARK

THE HIKE: Begin south-southwest from the parking area, keep straight at the dam, and traverse an open side slope with Stillwater Reservoir on your left. After 0.7 mile from the trailhead, take the left fork at signs and a trail register. You are now on the Bear River Trail (Number 1120). Pass through some more open meadow before entering the forest as the trail curves to the right and soon reaches Mosquito Lake, which is in a large bowl with the Devils Causeway visible to the northwest. Many trees in the area have been defoliated by a bark beetle infestation, which is said to have occurred over 40 years ago. The trail continues on toward several possible destinations, including Trappers Lake and the Devils Causeway.

SEE MAP PAGE 111

50. Hooper Lake and Keener Lake

ROUND-TRIP DISTANCE	3.4 miles to Hooper Lake, 0.6 miles further to Keener Lake, total 8 miles
HIKING TIME	Out to Hooper Lake in 97 minutes, over to Keener Lake in 15 minutes, back in 98 minutes
STARTING ELEVATION	10,300 feet
HIGHEST ELEVATION	11,160 feet
ELEVATION GAIN	1,570 feet (includes 710 extra feet)
DIFFICULTY	Moderate
MAPS	Trails Illustrated, Flat Tops NE/Trappers Lake, Number 122 Dome Peak 7.5 minute Garfield County Number 1 Routt National Forest White River National Forest

COMMENT: In the second half of July, this hike in the Flat Tops Wilderness will surround you with wildflowers, especially lupine. The different terrain and two pristine lakes are three more reasons why this remote area is so popular.

GETTING THERE: On Colorado 131 drive to Yampa, which is north of Interstate 70 and south of Steamboat Springs. From Yampa take Garfield County Road 7, which becomes Forest Road 900, and drive 16.7 miles until the road ends at the trailhead and Stillwater Reservoir. Regular cars can reach the parking area at the road end.

THE HIKE: From the parking area at the end of Road 900, start walking on the trail to the south-southwest and quickly go left (south-southeast) on the Derby Trail, which crosses the dam above Stillwater Reservoir, before passing a trail register and plunging into the forest. The good trail passes a few ponds en route to a scenic open ridge at 11,160 feet. Then descend almost a mile through meadows to Hooper Lake off the trail on the right. The trail continues another 350 yards to a fork. Hike to the right (south) and reach Keener Lake in 0.4 mile from Hooper Lake. An impressive waterfall descends from the flat tops into the lake. Derby Peak can be seen to the south. Count your blessings, relax, and enjoy before returning as you came.

Hooper Lake.

PHOTO BY DAVE MULLER

SEE MAP PAGE 111

51. Wall Lake

ROUND-TRIP DISTANCE	8.8 miles
HIKING TIME	Up in 104 minutes, down in 85 minutes
STARTING ELEVATION	9,755 feet
HIGHEST ELEVATION	10,986 feet
ELEVATION GAIN	1,451 feet (includes an extra 110 feet each way)
DIFFICULTY	Moderate
MAPS	Trails Illustrated, Flat Tops NE/Trappers Lake, Number 122 Trappers Lake 7.5 minute Big Marvine Peak 7.5 minute Garfield County Number 1 White River National Forest

COMMENT: The Flat Tops Wilderness is a vast, lush area with many lakes, peaks, and trails. The trails often ascend from the valleys to broad, level expanses, known as flat tops, at 10,000 and 11,000 feet. In addition to many campgrounds, there are a few lodges at the margins of the wilderness. This hike to Wall Lake will give you a good taste of this vast public playground.

GETTING THERE: From the northern edge of the town of Yampa on Colorado 131, turn west onto Routt County Road 17 and set your mileage to zero. Continue straight at mile 4.4 and turn left at a sign at mile 5.5. Stay on the main road. Keep right at mile 5.7 and again at mile 12.4. Cross Dunckley Pass at mile 19.6, turn left at mile 26.8, and pass Vaughn Lake Campground, on the left at mile 34.3. Cross Ripple Creek Pass at mile 37.3, continue

Wall Lake.   PHOTO BY BOB WATKINS

straight at mile 37.7, and take a left fork at a sign at mile 43.0. At mile 50.7, take a right fork at a sign directing you to the Wall Lake trailhead. Continue straight at mile 51.7 and park in a cul-de-sac on the right, at the trailhead at mile 52.3. Regular cars can reach this point.

THE HIKE: Begin on foot to the south-southeast on a good trail that leads through the trees and up the valley. Quickly pass a wilderness sign and before long ascend a number of switchbacks to reach the mesa. You have come 3 miles and the vistas are now extensive. Take a left fork at a trail sign and traverse essentially open terrain the final 1.4 miles to the welcoming waters of Wall Lake. Trappers Peak rises to the southwest. The "Chinese Wall" lies to the north-northeast. Return by your ascent route. Trappers Lake will be visible to the north-northeast as you come down from the plateau.

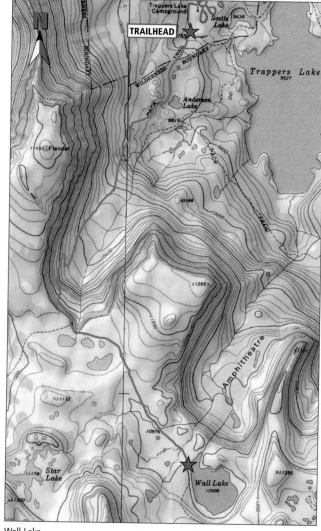

Wall Lake.

52. Lily Pad Lake (From Ryan Gulch Road)

ROUND-TRIP DISTANCE	3.4 miles
HIKING TIME	Up in 44 minutes, down in 44 minutes
STARTING ELEVATION	9,800 feet
HIGHEST ELEVATION	10,040 feet
ELEVATION GAIN	765 feet (includes 525 extra feet)
DIFFICULTY	Easy
MAPS	Trails Illustrated, Vail/Frisco/Dillon, Number 108 Frisco 7.5 minute Summit County Number 2 Arapaho National Forest – Dillon Ranger District

COMMENT: Lily Pad Lake is part of the Eagles Nest Wilderness. This small lake can be reached from the Ryan Gulch Road, as in this hike, from the frontage road parallel to Interstate 70 at the Breckenridge and Frisco exit (exit 203), or from the Wildernest Road via the Salt Lick Trail. The trail from the Ryan Gulch Road is popular and easy. It crosses a pretty forest and some small meadows before reaching a pond on the left and, in 75 more yards, beautiful Lily Pad Lake with Peak One visible to the south and Buffalo Mountain hovering above to the northwest.

GETTING THERE: Take exit 205 from Interstate 70 and drive north on Colorado 9 for 100 yards and turn left onto Wildernest Road and set your odometer to zero. Follow Wildernest Road, which becomes Ryan Gulch

Lake lily pads.   PHOTO BY ALAN STARK

Lily Pad Lake.

Road, for 3.4 miles and park in an open area on the left before the road begins to descend.

THE HIKE: From the parking area, walk south alongside the road and in 50 yards take the dirt road ascending to the right. Go around a barrier to vehicles and ascend the wide road 0.1 mile. At a level area, keep right and enter the woods at several signs. The trail then meanders past a pond on the right and proceeds up and down generally to the south. After 1.2 miles, keep right at a junction with the Salt Lick Trail and soon pass to the right of a small pond just before reaching Lily Pad Lake. A primitive 0.5 mile trail circles the lake. Enjoy it all before returning on the ascent route.

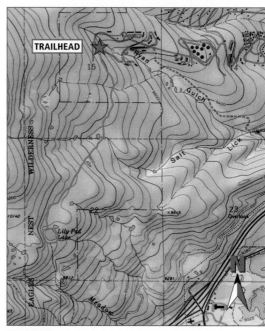

Lily Pad Lake.

119

53. Salmon Lake

ROUND-TRIP DISTANCE	15.4 miles
HIKING TIME	Up in 194 minutes, down in 170 minutes
STARTING ELEVATION	9,500 feet
HIGHEST ELEVATION	11,260 feet
ELEVATION GAIN	3,630 feet (includes 1,870 extra feet)
DIFFICULTY	More difficult
MAPS	Trails Illustrated, Vail/Frisco/Dillon, Number 108 Willow Lakes 7.5 minute Summit County Number 1 Arapaho National Forest – Dillon Ranger District

COMMENT: Salmon Lake is a beautiful hiking destination in the Eagles Nest Wilderness. The route uses part of the Gore Range Trail and is lengthy. Allow yourself adequate time to enjoy the lake and relax before the long way back.

The Gore Range Trail runs about 50 miles along the eastern flank of the Gore Range. Other long trails in Colorado include the Rainbow Trail in the Sangre de Cristo Mountains, the Continental Divide Trail, running north and south the length of the state and, of course, the Colorado Trail from Denver to Durango.

GETTING THERE: Drive north on Colorado 9 from Interstate 70 (exit 205) at Silverthorne for 7.9 miles. Then turn left and ascend Summit County Road 1350. This turnoff is opposite the Blue River Campground. After 1.4 miles on this side road, turn left onto the Rock Creek Road. Stay on this good dirt road and keep right at 0.4 miles, 1.1 miles, and at 1.4 miles. The last fork leads you into a parking area and the Rock Creek Trailhead as the road ends in a loop. Regular cars can reach this trailhead.

THE HIKE: From the trailhead, proceed south past a register and continue up around a road barrier. After 0.3 mile, at a sign, go left on the Gore Range Trail. Descend to a crossing of North Rock Creek. Continue south on the good, clear trail, which is marked by many tree cuts and an occasional sign. The trail rises and falls through mostly sparse forest, past occasional small pools, crosses South Rock Creek on a bridge, and then rises to cross over an aqueduct. Soon there is an unnamed lake on the right with mountains visible beyond. This lake is often full of water lilies and deserves a name.

Salmon Lake.

PHOTO BY MATHEW RICK

After 5.4 miles, you reach a fork at a Gore Range Trail sign. Go up the unmarked trail on the right (south-southwest). After 1.8 miles of mostly ascent, go right at an unmarked fork for the last 0.5 mile to Salmon Lake, with impressive rocky peaks to the south and west. (The left fork ascends the valley another 1.5 miles to the Willow Lakes, north of Red Peak.)

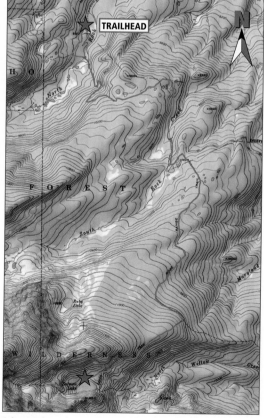

Salmon Lake.

54. Surprise Lake, Upper Cataract Lake, and Cat Lake

ROUND-TRIP DISTANCE	11.6 miles
HIKING TIME	Up in 145 minutes, down in 135 minutes
STARTING ELEVATION	8,580 feet
HIGHEST ELEVATION	10,850 feet
ELEVATION GAIN	2,850 feet (includes 580 extra feet)
DIFFICULTY	More difficult
MAPS	Trails Illustrated, Green Mountain Reservoir/Ute Pass, Number 107 Mount Powell 7.5 minute Summit County Number 1 Arapaho National Forest – Dillon Ranger District

COMMENT: Upper Cataract Lake drains by a waterfall into Cat Lake. A cataract is a large waterfall. These photogenic lakes lie in the Eagles Nest Wilderness. In season, the vegetation along this hike is very lush and the aspen are abundant. The route involves part of the Gore Range Trail, which runs north to south from the Green Mountain Reservoir area to Wheeler Junction, near Copper Mountain.

GETTING THERE: From Interstate 70 at Dillon and Silverthorne (exit 205), drive northwest on Colorado 9 for 16.7 miles and turn left onto Summit County Road 30. Follow this paved road to the left of Green Mountain Reservoir for 5.6 miles and turn sharply left and ascend Summit County Road 1725 for 2.3 miles to a sign and a fork. Go left another few hundred yards and park on the left at the Surprise Lake Trailhead. To reach this point, stay on the good main road (1725). Regular cars can readily reach this parking area.

THE HIKE: Proceed south by trail from the parking area. Cross Cataract Creek on a bridge and then ascend into the trees through an open fence. Stay on the good, main trail as it ascends past an occasional meadow and around a few fallen logs. After 2.7 miles, you will reach a junction with the Gore Range Trail and some signs. Go right (west) and soon reach lovely, small Surprise Lake on your left. Continue another 0.7 mile to another fork with signs. The right fork continues to Tipperary Lake, but you take the left fork west-northwest and follow the Cataract Trail. It will be another 2 miles from

Surprise Lake and its usual lily pads.

PHOTO BY DAVE COOPER

this fork to your destination. The trail crosses a ridge and descends over 200 feet to both lakes, which are connected by side trails. Upper Cataract Lake is dominated by the rugged slopes of Eagles Nest Mountain immediately to the south and supplies the lower, Cat Lake. The main trail continues on to Mirror Lake and beyond, but this is your turnaround point. Enjoy both of these lovely lakes before the return on your ascent route.

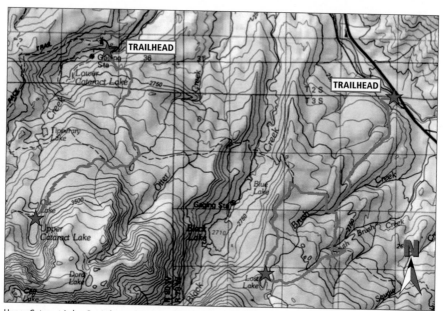

Upper Cataract Lake, Cat Lake, and Surprise Lake (left). Lost Lake (right).

55. Lost Lake (Upper Summit County)

ROUND-TRIP DISTANCE	6.2 miles on ascent, 6.3 miles on descent (Total loop 12.5 miles)
HIKING TIME	Up in 170 minutes, down in 153 minutes
STARTING ELEVATION	8,110 feet
HIGHEST ELEVATION	10,155 feet
ELEVATION GAIN	2,630 feet (includes 585 extra feet)
DIFFICULTY	More difficult
MAPS	Trails Illustrated, Green Mountain Reservoir/Ute Pass, Number 107 Squaw Creek 7.5 minute Mount Powell 7.5 minute Summit County Number 1 Arapaho National Forest – Dillon Ranger District

COMMENT: Of the many routes to "Lost Lakes" in Colorado, this hike is one of the most enjoyable and most demanding, unless you can access the trailhead by four-wheel-drive vehicle. This outing uses a loop trail off the Gore Range Trail. A clockwise direction will be described. The Gore Range Trail runs north and south along the eastern edge of the Gore Range. Over 54 miles in length, this pathway extends from near Mahan Lake on the north to Wheeler Flats on the south. Virtually all of this hike lies within the Eagles Nest Wilderness, with many aspen groves along the way.

GETTING THERE: From Interstate 70 at Silverthorne, take exit 205 and drive north on Colorado 9 for 16.6 miles and turn left onto Summit County Road 30. After 0.5 mile on this road, park off road as a steep side road ascends on the left. (If you have four-wheel-drive and good clearance, you can drive 1.8 miles on this rough road to a fork. Continue driving up left for 0.6 mile further to the trailhead as the road ends. You will have saved over 1,000 feet of elevation gain as well as the 2.4 miles each way.)

THE HIKE: Begin generally south and then west up the rocky Brush Creek Road, which winds steeply upward, to reach a fork at mile 1.6. Keep left another 0.8 mile to a trailhead register and sign. Pass through a fence to the south and hike through a high, open meadow on a side slope with Brush Creek below on your left. Enter the forest near a wilderness sign and reach a signed fork after 0.5 mile from the trailhead. Descend left (east) to a creek crossing and continue through the forest on the Gore Range Trail for 1.2

Lost Lake.

PHOTO BY DARREN LINGLE

miles to another fork and a small sign on a tree. Ascend to the right (south) on the Lost Lake Trail. The trail crosses a creek and leads generally west. If you lose the trail, head toward the slopes on the right side of Guyselman Mountain, which is visible to the southwest.

Lost Lake is rather large, with the high summits of the Gore Range above to the west and southwest. Dora Mountain is prominent to the west-southwest. A faint trail continues along the right (north) side of the lake and then becomes more defined as it curves down to the right for 2.1 miles to intersect with the Gore Range Trail. Take the right fork to the south-southeast, pass through two meadows and reach the end of the loop in another 1.2 miles. From this intersection, continue straight back to the trailhead, the rough road and your vehicle.

SEE MAP PAGE 123

56. Old Dillon Reservoir

ROUND-TRIP DISTANCE	1.2 miles
HIKING TIME	Up in 13 minutes, down in 11 minutes
STARTING ELEVATION	9,080 feet
HIGHEST ELEVATION	9,300 feet
ELEVATION GAIN	325 feet (includes 105 extra feet)
DIFFICULTY	Easy
MAPS	Trails Illustrated, Vail/Frisco/Dillon, Number 108 Frisco 7.5 minute Summit County Number 2 Arapaho National Forest – Dillon Ranger District

COMMENT: This short, scenic hike to the Old Dillon Reservoir lies between Lake Dillon and Interstate 70. The good views from the ridge in the middle part of this hike are special. Buffalo Mountain, Torreys Peak, Grays Peak, Mount Guyot, Bald Mountain, and the Tenmile Range encircle the route.

GETTING THERE: Drive south from exit 203 of Interstate 70 west of Dillon, and within 100 yards turn left onto the frontage road, also called the Dam Road. Follow this paved road to the northeast for 1.8 miles and turn left into the parking area at the Old Dillon Reservoir trailhead.

Old Dillon Reservoir.   PHOTO BY CLIF REED

Old Dillon Reservoir.

PHOTO BY CLIF REED

THE HIKE: Begin to the west-northwest from the trailhead sign and follow the good trail up to the ridge. Lake Dillon is impressive on the right. Follow the ridge down to the former reservoir and avoid a trail descending on your left from the ridge. A trail circles the reservoir over 0.3 mile and connects back to the ridge trail and the trailhead.

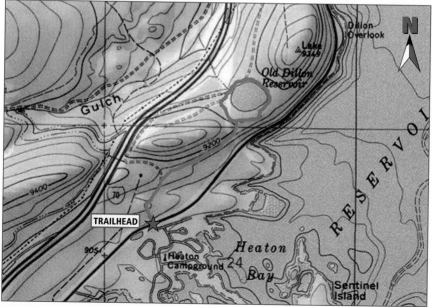

Old Dillon Reservoir.

127

57. Wheeler Lakes

ROUND-TRIP DISTANCE	7.0 miles
HIKING TIME	Up in 100 minutes, down in 80 minutes
STARTING ELEVATION	9,660 feet
HIGHEST ELEVATION	11,080 feet
ELEVATION GAIN	1,515 feet (includes 95 extra feet)
DIFFICULTY	Moderate
MAPS	Trails Illustrated, Vail/Frisco/Dillon, Number 108 Vail Pass 7.5 minute Summit County Number 2 Arapaho National Forest – Dillon Ranger District

COMMENT: These lakes, Wheeler Flats, the ghost town of Wheeler, the Wheeler Trail, Wheeler Peak, and Wheeler Lake to the south, are all named after Judge John S. Wheeler, a rancher in this area in the latter 1800s.

The convenient trailhead and gradual ascent north of the Copper Mountain Ski Area make this a good family hike. The Wheeler Lakes are only a few hundred yards apart and can usually be reached by hikers from the second half of June through October.

GETTING THERE: Drive west on Interstate 70 4.8 miles past exit 201 and park in the lot on the right (north).

THE HIKE: Start on the trail south-southwest from the parking area; go left and follow the main trail as it parallels Interstate 70, and curves right before ascending into the trees. Stay on the good main trail and reach the Eagles Nest Wilderness after 1.6 miles. Pass through an aspen grove. Continue generally northwest and at mile 3.2 reach a fork marked by a sign. Go to the right and enter an open area. (The left fork is the Gore Range Trail and leads past Lost Lake to Uneva Pass and beyond.) Within 0.3 mile, you will reach the two Wheeler Lakes, each to the right of the trail. Above the second lake, to the north, there is a fine overlook at a saddle, with Buffalo Mountain visible to the north, Dillon to the north-northeast, Uneva Pass to the northwest, and Peak One to the east-northeast. The trail fades away beyond the lakes. Return as you ascended with good views of the Copper Mountain Ski Area and the Tenmile Range.

One of the Wheeler Lakes.

PHOTO BY DAVE MULLER

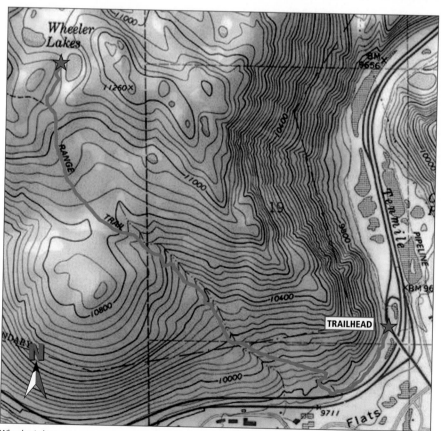

Wheeler Lakes.

58. Crystal Lake

ROUND-TRIP DISTANCE	2.8 miles
HIKING TIME	Out in 34 minutes, back in 30 minutes
STARTING ELEVATION	11,539 feet
HIGHEST ELEVATION	11,735 feet
ELEVATION GAIN	309 feet (includes 113 extra feet)
DIFFICULTY	Easy
MAPS	Trails Illustrated, Breckenridge/Tennessee Pass, Number 109 Alma 7.5 minute Summit County Number 2 Arapaho National Forest – Dillon Ranger District

COMMENT: This easy outing uses an old mining road just below timberline en route to an obscure lake just below some extensive mine remnants. The views of Quandary Peak, a Fourteener, down to Lake Dillon and across the valley to the east, are special. The gradual grade and short length make this especially suitable for families and out-of-state visitors.

GETTING THERE: Drive on Colorado 9 to Hoosier Pass, between Breckenridge on the north and Fairplay to the south. Park on the west side of the pass in the large area behind the Hoosier Pass sign.

THE HIKE: Begin west-northwest up the wide, rough road from Hoosier Pass. Follow the road for 100 yards as it curves up and left to a fork. Here you go to the right (north) as the road passes below a few trees at timberline, with

Crystal Lake.　　　　　PHOTO BY DAVE COOPER

Crystal Lake.

PHOTO BY DAVE COOPER

wonderful scenery. Quandary Peak can be seen to the northwest. After a high point on the road, there is a gradual decline to another fork. Here the road on the left is blocked to vehicles. You continue on the right fork (northwest),

cross the outlet of Crystal Lake, and reach the lake within 60 more yards. I saw no evidence of fish in the clear water. The ridge to the west belongs to North Star Mountain. The road continues to the site of an old mine and beyond to the northwest.

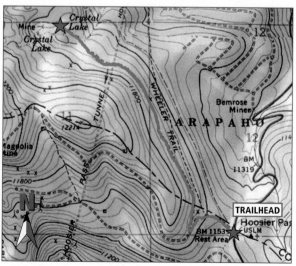

Crystal Lake.

59. Kite Lake and Lake Emma

ROUND-TRIP DISTANCE	1.4 miles to Kite Lake, 1.0 mile further to Lake Emma (Total 2.4 miles each way) Round-trip 4.8 miles
HIKING TIME	35 minutes up to Kite Lake, 30 more minutes to Lake Emma, down in 50 minutes
STARTING ELEVATION	11,350 feet
HIGHEST ELEVATION	12,630 feet
ELEVATION GAIN	1,350 feet (includes 35 feet extra each way)
DIFFICULTY	Moderate
MAPS	Trails Illustrated, Breckenridge/Tennessee Pass, Number 109 Climax 7.5 minute Alma 7.5 minute Park County Number 1 Pike National Forest

COMMENT: This hike starts at an abandoned mine and ascends an old road to Kite Lake, which is bordered on three sides by Mount Democrat, Mount Cameron, and Mount Bross. All are over 14,000 feet high. Then leave the majority of hikers climbing Mount Democrat and ascend southwest to rugged Lake Emma at the southeast foot of Mount Democrat.

GETTING THERE: From the town of Alma on Colorado 9, drive west on a dirt road, opposite the post office and a gas station for 4.2 miles. This road follows Buckskin Creek to the old Home Sweet Home Mine with its diggings and an abandoned brown building on the right. Park here. (The road

Lake Emma.

PHOTO BY GINNI GREER

Kite Lake.

PHOTO BY DAVE COOPER

continues up to Kite Lake but gets rougher past this point.) Regular cars can easily come this far.

THE HIKE: Start to the northwest up the road and cross a small creek before reaching lovely Kite Lake in 1.4 miles from your vehicle. This is a popular spot for camping and is the trailhead for Mount Democrat. For Lake Emma, take the faint trail leading southwest from the toilet on the southern edge of Kite Lake. The trail gets faint at times and crosses the outflow of Lake Emma before steeply rising to the rocky lake, which will have some ice on its surface into July. Mount Democrat looms above to the north-northwest. Return as you ascended.

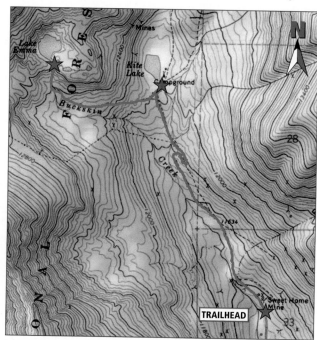

Lake Emma and Kite Lake.

60. Kroenke Lake

ROUND-TRIP DISTANCE	8.4 miles
HIKING TIME	Up in 114 minutes, down in 84 minutes
STARTING ELEVATION	9,840 feet
HIGHEST ELEVATION	11,530 feet
ELEVATION GAIN	2,200 feet (includes 510 extra feet)
DIFFICULTY	Moderate
MAPS	Trails Illustrated, Buena Vista/Collegiate Peaks, Number 129 Mount Yale 7.5 minute Chaffee County Number 2 San Isabel National Forest

COMMENT: Kroenke Lake lies close to three Fourteeners in the Collegiate Peaks Wilderness. These three are Mount Yale, Mount Harvard, and Mount Columbia. This popular hike begins at the North Cottonwood Creek trailhead and proceeds up to a fork. The left fork leads to Kroenke Lake and Browns Pass, and the trail on the right leads to lovely Horn Fork Basin, Bear Lake, and Mount Harvard.

GETTING THERE: From the middle of Buena Vista, at the intersection of U.S. 24 and Chaffee County Road 306, drive north on U.S. 24 for 0.4 mile and turn left (west) on Crossman Avenue, which is County Road 350. After 2.1 straight miles on this road, turn right onto Road 361. After 0.9 mile on Road 361, turn sharply left onto Road 365. Follow this main dirt road for 5.2 miles and park near the trailhead signboard at the end of the road. Regular cars can reach this point on the occasionally rough road. (Road 361 and Road 365 can also be reached from Road 306 and several other connecting county roads west of U.S. 24.)

THE HIKE: Begin walking west on the good path, which quickly passes a trail register and follows North Cottonwood Creek. A bridge crossing

Kroenke Lake. PHOTO BY KEITH JENSEN

Kroenke Lake.

PHOTO BY KEITH JENSEN

occurs before you arrive at a sign and a fork almost 2 miles from the trailhead. Take the left fork to the west, as the right fork ascends into Horn Fork Basin. The trail becomes somewhat steeper as it rises through the forest and makes two creek crossings. The second creek drains the basin below Birthday Peak.

The final approach becomes more gradual before Kroenke Lake comes into view. A short descent brings you to the edge of the lake, which has an island in its center. The trail continues southwest up to Browns Pass and beyond. The high peaks around Kroenke Lake are impressive. Mount Yale is prominent to the southeast and Birthday peak can barely be seen to the north. Take your time at this scenic lake before your return.

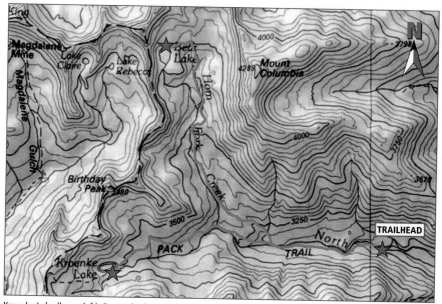

Kroenke Lake (lower left). Bear Lake (upper center).

61. Bear Lake (Chaffee County)

ROUND-TRIP DISTANCE	10.4 miles
HIKING TIME	Up in 104 minutes, down in 75 minutes
STARTING ELEVATION	9,840 feet
HIGHEST ELEVATION	12,400 feet
ELEVATION GAIN	3,040 feet (includes 240 extra feet each way)
DIFFICULTY	More difficult
MAPS	Trails Illustrated, Buena Vista/Collegiate Peaks, Number 129 Mount Harvard 7.5 minute Mount Yale 7.5 minute Chaffee County Numbers 1 and 2 San Isabel National Forest

COMMENT: This Bear Lake, surrounded by three Fourteeners (Mount Harvard, Mount Columbia, and Mount Yale), is even more scenic than the very popular lake of the same name in Rocky Mountain National Park. The trail to Bear Lake follows the drainage of the Horn Fork of North Cottonwood Creek in the Collegiate Peaks Wilderness. Horn Fork Basin is one of the most beautiful in Colorado.

GETTING THERE: From central Buena Vista at the intersection of U.S. 24 and Chaffee County Road 306 (The Cottonwood Pass Road), drive north on U.S. 24 for 0.4 mile and turn left (west) on Crossman Avenue, which is County Road 350. After 2.1 straight miles on this road, turn right at a T onto County Road 365. Follow this main dirt road for 5.2 miles and park at the trailhead as the road ends. Regular cars can reach this point.

THE HIKE: From the parking area and trailhead sign, proceed to the west. Pass a trail register, cross a bridge, and continue through the woods for 1.3 miles to a signed fork. The left trail leads to Kroenke Lake and Browns Pass. You take the right fork and ascend west-northwest into Horn Fork Basin. After 2.2 miles from this fork, you will emerge into a lovely bowl near timberline. Mount Columbia rises on the right and Mount Harvard to the north at the head of the valley. Continue north-northwest another 1.5 miles to a bench above some willows and a trail fork. The right fork ascends Mount Harvard. Continue straight (west) over a small creek and reach Bear Lake in 0.25 mile.

Bear Lake from Mount Harvard trail.   PHOTO BY CLAIRE BOW

When viewed from above, this lake has the contours of a bearskin rug. The Continental Divide lies to the west. Mount Columbia is located to the east, at the end of a long ridge. The Mount Harvard summit is partially obscured to the north-northwest by a rocky sub-peak. Mount Yale can be seen down the valley to the south-southeast.

Enjoy the privilege of being in such an exalted location before returning by your ascent route.

SEE MAP PAGE 135

62. Cow Lake

ROUND-TRIP DISTANCE	5.6 miles
HIKING TIME	Up in 85 minutes, down in 60 minutes
STARTING ELEVATION	10,680 feet
HIGHEST ELEVATION	11,417 feet
ELEVATION GAIN	1,649 feet (includes 912 extra feet)
DIFFICULTY	Moderate
MAPS	Trails Illustrated, Buena Vista/Collegiate Peaks, Number 129 Tincup 7.5 minute Gunnison County Number 3 Gunnison Basin Area – Gunnison National Forest

COMMENT: With cows and beef so important to Colorado's economy, it is surprising that there are not more "Cow" Lakes. This route is infrequently used and parallels Cow Creek after leaving the Timberline Trail. Serene Cow Lake lies below several unnamed peaks on the Continental Divide.

GETTING THERE: On Chaffee Road 306, drive west for 19 miles from U.S. 24 and Main Street in Buena Vista to Cottonwood Pass. The road to the pass from Buena Vista is paved. Continue down from Cottonwood Pass on the good, wide gravel road for 6.0 more miles and turn left into the parking area for the Timberline Trail.

THE HIKE: Begin on the narrow trail leading east from the parking area. Within 40 yards, pass a trail register and cross Pass Creek. Much of this hike is shaded, due to the thick forest. The trail rises and falls along a shelf. Pass through a small meadow before reaching Cow Creek after 1.3 miles from the trailhead.

Here is the key intersection of this hike: just before a crossing of Cow Creek, ascend east on an obscure trail on the left. Follow this trail with Cow Creek always on your right. Pass some ponds and ascend more steeply for the final 0.5 mile to the small lake in a bowl beneath the Continental Divide to the southeast. The southern edge of the lake is bounded by a steep rocky wall, and the outlet is in the southwest corner. The trees to the east ascend gently to the long ridge of the Divide. On your return, be sure to turn right when you join the Timberline Trail.

Cow Lake.

PHOTO BY CATHY McKEEN

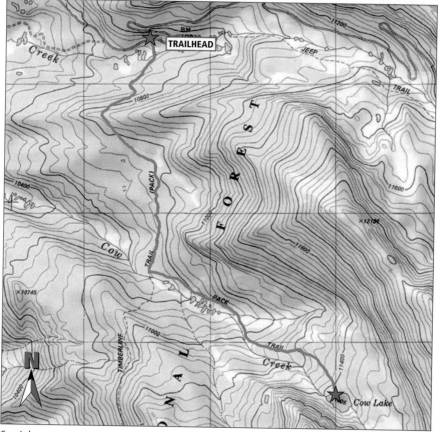

Cow Lake.

63. Henry Lake

ROUND-TRIP DISTANCE	15 miles
HIKING TIME	Up in 205 minutes, down in 158 minutes.
STARTING ELEVATION	9,200 feet
HIGHEST ELEVATION	11,704 feet
ELEVATION GAIN	3,048 feet (includes 272 extra feet each way)
DIFFICULTY	More difficult
MAPS	Trails Illustrated, Crested Butte/Pearl Pass, Number 131, and Gunnison/Pitkin, Number 132 Taylor Park Reservoir 7.5 minute Fairview Peak 7.5 minute Gunnison County Number 3 Gunnison National Forest

COMMENT: This remote and lengthy hike rewards with a beautiful lake just below treeline, abundant aspen in the initial third, and an excellent, sometimes rocky trail in the Fossil Ridge Wilderness. This is a popular horse trail.

GETTING THERE: From Buena Vista on Main Street (U.S. 24) drive west at the stoplight on County Road 306 over Cottonwood Pass on the good road to Taylor Park Reservoir. Go left on road 742 at the end of the Cottonwood Pass Road and drive around the left side of the Taylor Park Reservoir on Road 742, which is called the Taylor River Road. 3.7 miles west of the Taylor Park Dam turn left onto the Lottis Creek Campground. Continue straight another 0.5 mile and park at the South Lottis Creek Trailhead.

THE HIKE: Start out to the south-southeast through an unlocked gate. After 0.2 mile go right and leave the road at a sign. Cross Lottis Creek on logs and continue gradually up the valley with South Lottis Creek on your right. After about 5 miles take a right fork (south) and continue up into a basin with a boulder field on the left. The gradual tail becomes very steep for the final 0.3 mile to Henry Lake, with Henry Mountain above to the south southwest.

Henry Lake and Henry Mountain.

PHOTO BY DAVE MULLER

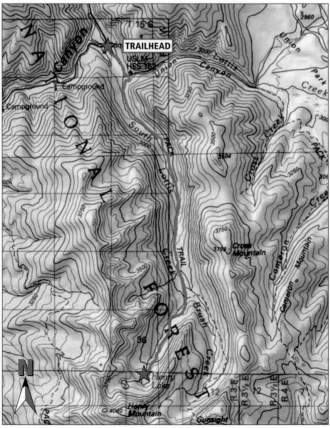

Henry Lake.

64. Pomeroy Lake and Upper Pomeroy Lake

ROUND-TRIP DISTANCE	8.2 miles
HIKING TIME	Up in 115 minutes, down in 90 minutes
STARTING ELEVATION	10,563 feet
HIGHEST ELEVATION	12,270 feet
ELEVATION GAIN	1,947 feet (includes 120 extra feet each way)
DIFFICULTY	Moderate
MAPS	Trails Illustrated, Salida/St. Elmo/Mount Shavano, Number 130 Saint Elmo 7.5 minute Chaffee County Numbers 2 and 3 San Isabel National Forest

COMMENT: Not many hikers ascend Pomeroy Gulch. Some fishermen and four-wheel-drivers, however, may be encountered. En route to the two lakes at the head of the valley, many mine remnants are present. Especially extensive are the leavings of the Mary Murphy Mine, which a grateful mine owner named after a Denver nurse.

The rough road climbs up the valley and becomes rougher shortly before it is blocked adjacent to Pomeroy Lake.

GETTING THERE: From U.S. 285, south of Buena Vista, drive west on Chaffee County Road 162. Stay on this road for 15.4 miles to a fork, just before entering the historic town of Saint Elmo. Ascend the left fork, which is Chaffee Road 295. This road leads to the ghost towns of Romley and Hancock, and beyond. Follow this dirt road for 2.9 miles to a sign indicating that the left fork leads to the Mary Murphy Mine and the Pomeroy Lakes. Park here off the road.

THE HIKE: Start steeply on foot up the side road. The grade levels out as you pass through the old Mary Murphy Mine, 1 mile from your trailhead. The open valley beckons ahead. After passing through a treeless area, enter the trees and arrive at a fork. The left fork ascends to the upper areas of Chrysolite Mountain. You continue straight ahead. Soon, pass an old grave off of the right side of the road. About 300 yards past this grave, take a left fork and continue your ascent. (The right fork leads quickly to an old mine cabin.) Follow the wide road up to a grassy bench, where the road is blocked

Upper Pomeroy Lake.

PHOTO BY RICK SCHROEDER

and where Pomeroy Lake can be seen below on your right. A faint trail leads 150 yards to the edge of the lake. To gain Upper Pomeroy Lake, which is cradled in a cirque, continue south on the overgrown road. Lose a little elevation before reaching this very high lake at the foot of Pomeroy Mountain to the south-southeast. A trail can be seen rising to the ridge above the left side of the lake. Return as you ascended. On clear days, Mount Yale is visible to the north from the upper basin.

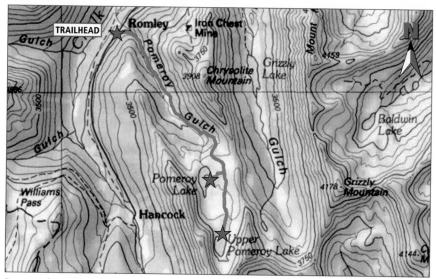

Pomeroy Lake and Upper Pomeroy Lake.

65. Baldwin Lake

ROUND-TRIP DISTANCE	10.2 miles
HIKING TIME	Up in 170 minutes, down in 105 minutes
STARTING ELEVATION	9,420 feet
HIGHEST ELEVATION	12,088 feet
ELEVATION GAIN	3,008 feet (includes 340 extra feet)
DIFFICULTY	More difficult
MAPS	Trails Illustrated, Salida/St. Elmo/Mount Shavano, Number 130 St. Elmo 7.5 minute Chaffee County Numbers 2 and 3 San Isabel National Forest

COMMENT: Baldwin Lake lies in a valley off of the most popular hiking route up Mount Antero, one of Colorado's wonderful Fourteeners. This might explain why this lake is often overlooked. It lies above timberline in a vast basin ringed by high peaks, near the end of an old mining road that can be driven with a four-wheel-drive vehicle to within a short walk to the lake.

GETTING THERE: From the junction with U.S. Highway 24, south of Buena Vista, drive south on U.S. 285 for 5.5 miles. Then turn right (west) on Chaffee County Road 162. Follow this good road for 12.3 miles to a sign indicating that Mount Antero and Baldwin Lake can be reached on the road that ascends left. (This rough road requires four-wheel-drive and high clearance.) Park off of Road 162, near this side road.

THE HIKE: Begin on foot up the rough road to the southeast. With Baldwin Creek always on your left, ascend through the forest. Stay on the main road and avoid any side roads on the right. At mile 2.8, you reach a fork and signs. (The left fork road crosses Baldwin Creek and continues toward Mount Antero.) You continue straight (southwest) past a signboard on the rough road. Pass a grassy meadow on the left and shortly thereafter a talus slope on the right. There are few trees as you rise in the basin. At mile 4.7, the road splits. Descend to the left (south). (The right fork curves up to an old mine.) Pass several unnamed ponds below timberline on the left before reaching a small parking area on the left, around treeline at mile 5.5. From this area follow a footpath to the southwest as it snakes the last 300 yards to Baldwin Lake and a sign. Boulder Mountain lies north. Mount Antero can

Baldwin Lake.

PHOTO BY RICK SCHROEDER

be seen back to the northeast. Cyclone Mountain hovers to the south-southwest, Grizzly Mountain to the south-southeast, and Mount Mamma to the west-northwest. Enjoy it all and return by your ascent route.

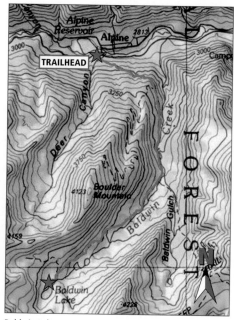

Baldwin Lake.

145

66. Hunt Lake

ROUND-TRIP DISTANCE	5.8 miles
HIKING TIME	Up in 85 minutes, down in 60 minutes
STARTING ELEVATION	9,950 feet
HIGHEST ELEVATION	11,535 feet
ELEVATION GAIN	1,835 feet (includes 125 extra feet each way)
DIFFICULTY	Moderate
MAPS	Trails Illustrated, Salida/St. Elmo/Mount Shavano, Number 130 Garfield 7.5 minute Chaffee County Number 3 San Isabel National Forest

COMMENT: Lying in the shadow of the Continental Divide, tranquil Hunt Lake is reached by a rough old mining road that uses part of the Continental Divide Trail. This area in lower Chaffee County is not heavily used. There are no restrictions on pets or bicycles.

GETTING THERE: West of Salida, drive on U.S. 50, either west for 13.2 miles from the intersection with U.S. 285 North, or east for 4.2 miles from Monarch Pass. Then turn north on unpaved Forest Road 235. Drive 0.2 mile to a four-way intersection and park nearby off the road.

THE HIKE: Begin up the left (west) fork and ascend the rough four-wheel-drive road (Road 235), which continues through the forest for 1.6 miles to a four-

Hunt Lake.   PHOTO BY CATHY McKEEN

Hunt Lake.

PHOTO BY CATHY McKEEN

way intersection, with the Boss Lake Reservoir below to the west. Within 125 yards, take the left (south) fork on a road that is blocked to vehicles. Continue on the road, which is part of the Continental Divide Trail. The grade is moderate for the last 1.2 miles to Hunt Lake on the right. Shortly before reaching the lake, you pass an inviting meadow on the right. From Hunt Lake, Clover Mountain is the prominent peak to the northwest. Bald Mountain is to the west-southwest and Banana Mountain looms close above to the south. The trail continues up to the ridge and the Continental Divide.

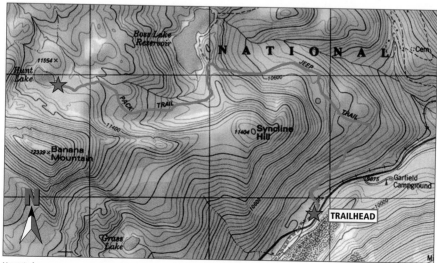

Hunt Lake.

67. Peanut Lake and Cherry Lake

ROUND-TRIP DISTANCE	11 miles
HIKING TIME	Up in 155 minutes, down in 110 minutes
STARTING ELEVATION	8,535 feet
HIGHEST ELEVATION	11,810 feet
ELEVATION GAIN	4,000 feet (includes 725 extra feet)
DIFFICULTY	More difficult
MAPS	Trails Illustrated, Sangre de Cristo Mountains/Great Sand Dunes National Park, Number 138 Electric Peak 7.5 minute Rito Alto Peak 7.5 minute Mirage 7.5 minute Saguache County Numbers 2, 4, and 5 Rio Grande National Forest

COMMENT: Here is a hike in the beautiful Sangre de Cristo Wilderness, which was so designated in 1993. More usage of this area originates from Westcliffe and the Wet Mountain Valley, but this access from the more remote west can bring you to many good trails, lakes, and peaks. The trail to Peanut and Cherry Lakes follows the rushing waters of Wild Cherry Creek, up through an extensive aspen forest, and eventually into a higher grove of evergreens, before reaching the lakes at the foot of Mount Owen, a thirteener. Anytime from mid-June through September is the usual season for this outing, but the middle of September would be ideal due to the fall, golden colors of the aspen.

GETTING THERE: From Poncha Pass, south of Salida, drive south on U.S. 285 for 18.4 miles and turn left onto Colorado 17. Drive south on Colorado 17 for 6.2 miles and turn left onto unpaved Saguache County Road AA. (This point is marked as Mirage on some maps.) Follow Road AA to the east for 7.8 miles and take the right fork for 0.4 mile further to the trailhead and park. Most regular cars can reach this parking area.

Peanut Lake. PHOTO BY CATHY McKEEN

Cherry Lake.

PHOTO BY CATHY McKEEN

THE HIKE: Begin to the east from a signboard and follow Wild Cherry Creek, always on your right, up the basin. Many switchbacks provide relief from the steep ascent. After 2 miles, pass a wilderness sign and continue up to the north-northeast. A clearing is finally reached, with Mount Owen visible to the north. Cross the clearing by trail and switchback up into the evergreens before reaching a high point and your first views of your destination. Then descend 0.2 mile to smaller Peanut Lake and the larger Cherry Lake immediately to the southeast in a scenic rocky bowl. The trail ends here. The beauty of this upper basin will put extra bounce in your step as you return through the aspen back to the trailhead.

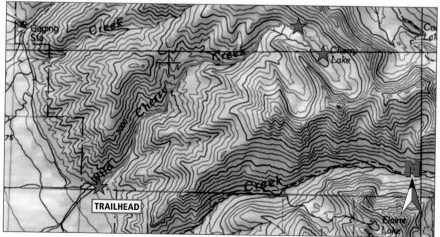

Peanut Lake and Cherry Lake.

68. West Tennessee Lakes

ROUND-TRIP DISTANCE	9.4 miles
HIKING TIME	Up in 120 minutes, down in 108 minutes
STARTING ELEVATION	10,420 feet
HIGHEST ELEVATION	11,835 feet
ELEVATION GAIN	1,685 feet (includes 135 extra feet each way)
DIFFICULTY	Moderate
MAPS	Trails Illustrated, Breckenridge/Tennessee Pass, Number 109, and Holy Cross/Ruedi Reservoir, Number 126 Leadville North 7.5 minute Homestake Reservoir 7.5 minute Lake County San Isabel National Forest

COMMENT: The two West Tennessee Lakes are located deep in a little-used but lovely mountain basin, west of Leadville.

Most of the route uses an old mining road. In its upper areas, within the Holy Cross Wilderness, the trail is faint and primitive at times. The flowing waters of West Tennessee Creek, the lakes, and the unspoiled valley make this a most rewarding hike.

GETTING THERE: From the intersection with Colorado 91 at the northern edge of Leadville, drive northwest on U.S. 24 toward Tennessee Pass. After 7.1 miles from Colorado 91, turn left, set your odometer to zero and follow the good, main dirt road to the west. Keep left after 0.9 mile and turn right at a fork at mile 1.3 from U.S. 24. Keep right again at a sign at mile 1.5 and once more at mile 1.6. Go straight at a four-way intersection at mile 1.8 and park off road at mile 2.2, just before a crossing of the North Fork of West Tennessee Creek. Most regular cars can reach this point. Four-wheel-drive is necessary for the next 0.5 mile, before a gate blocks the road.

THE HIKE: Start hiking over the creek and follow the rough road 0.5 mile to a four-way intersection. Lily Lake with its many water lilies is on the left. A trail to the 10th Mountain Hut, which can be rented, is on the right. You continue straight up the road and around a locked gate. The road becomes steeper before you emerge into a more level area, with a lovely meadow on your left. At mile 1.9 from your trailhead, pass through a wooden fence. Over sometimes marshy terrain, it is another mile to the Holy Cross Wilderness boundary and a trail register. Continue generally south-southwest with

Lower West Tennessee Lake.

PHOTO BY DAVE MULLER

the meadow and creek on your left. At 1.2 miles from the wilderness sign you reach a small, unnamed round lake on the right. Continue past the lake and follow an overgrown trail along the right side of the creek and then ascend more steeply for 0.5 mile, with the creek on your left, over an adequate trail to reach lower West Tennessee Lake. The faint trail then crosses the inlet creek and reaches the much larger upper lake on the left, after 0.2 mile. When weather conditions are good, this is an idyllic setting, with Galena Mountain and the Continental Divide to the south and Homestake Peak in the distance to the north. Not many Coloradoans visit these lakes. Savor the experience and return by your ascent trail.

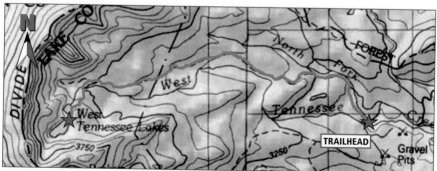

West Tennessee Lakes.

69. Windsor Lake

ROUND-TRIP DISTANCE	4 miles
HIKING TIME	Up in 60 minutes, down in 38 minutes
STARTING ELEVATION	10,790 feet
HIGHEST ELEVATION	11,638 feet
ELEVATION GAIN	990 feet (includes 142 total extra feet)
DIFFICULTY	Easy
MAPS	Trails Illustrated, Aspen/Independence Pass, Number 127 Mount Massive 7.5 minute Lake County San Isabel National Forest

COMMENT: Located within the Mount Massive Wilderness, beautiful Windsor Lake can be reached by two trails that begin at the Hagerman Pass Road. The clearer, northern route will be described here. It passes by a smaller, unnamed lake and reaches the eastern edge of Windsor Lake. The southern trail stays closer to Busk Creek, is hard to follow at times, and reaches the southern shore of Windsor Lake.

GETTING THERE: From the south side of Turquoise Lake, west of Leadville, drive on the bumpy, dirt road toward Hagerman Pass for 3.7 miles from the paved road around the lake. Park on the right, at the sign for Windsor Lake parking. Regular cars can reach this point.

THE HIKE: Begin to the south-southwest and, on a small bridge, cross the outflow from the old Carlton Tunnel. After a brief descent and curve to the left, cross a creek and ascend the right fork to the west-northwest. Pass a trail register and rise steeply into the trees. About halfway to your destination, the trail goes by a cave on the right and climbs steeply to an overlook of a lovely and smaller unnamed lake. There are good views behind you into the Busk Creek drainage. Continue by trail to the left of this lake, to a ridge with Windsor Lake a short distance below. The Continental Divide rises above to the west of this attractive lake. A return by your ascent route is recommended.

SIDEBAR: Mount Massive Wilderness Area

This 30,540 acre wilderness area is part of the Sawatch Range and was designated a wilderness by Congress in 1980.

Windsor Lake.

PHOTO BY CLIF REED

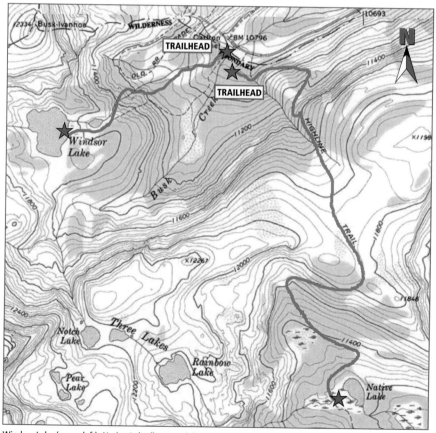

Windsor Lake (upper left). Native Lake (lower right).

70. Native Lake

ROUND-TRIP DISTANCE	7.4 miles
HIKING TIME	Out in 100 minutes, back in 85 minutes
STARTING ELEVATION	10,780 feet
HIGHEST ELEVATION	11,765 feet
ELEVATION GAIN	1,940 feet (includes 955 extra feet)
DIFFICULTY	Moderate
MAPS	Trails Illustrated, Aspen/Independence Pass, Number 127
	Mount Massive 7.5 minute
	Lake County
	San Isabel National Forest

COMMENT: Hiking to Native Lake will be a new experience for many. The lake is located in the Mount Massive Wilderness at the foot of Mount Massive, the second highest peak in Colorado. This area is not heavily used. The lush foliage, flowing creeks and the extensive tundra at timberline make this an especially scenic outing. Native Lake can also be reached by trail from the southeast, via the National Fish Hatchery and the Evergreen Lakes.

GETTING THERE: From Harrison Street in Leadville (U.S. 24), drive west on West 6th Street for 0.8 mile and then turn right. Bear left in another 0.1 mile, stay on the main, paved road and after 2.5 miles further take a right fork. Keep straight at an intersection after another 0.8 mile and pass to the left of huge Turquoise Lake, which will now be visible. After 3.4 more miles from the last intersection, leave the paved road and go left onto the wide road to Hagerman Pass. Follow this road for 3.6 miles and turn left at a sign and park at the Native Lake trailhead. Regular cars can reach this parking area, but the road is bumpy.

THE HIKE: From the parking area, ascend south past a trail register and signboard. Rise through the forest and several clearings with heavy vegetation. After a number of switchbacks and creek crossings, you will arrive at a large grassy mesa at timberline. The trail here is marked with a series of wooden poles supported by rocks at their base. As the trail begins to descend, you will soon see Native Lake below. The good, unambiguous trail continues down alongside the lake. A brief jaunt off trail to the left (east) brings you to the lake. There are good campsites in the trees around the lake. Take the same route back to the trailhead and "leave only footprints."

Native Lake.

PHOTO BY CLIF REED

SEE MAP PAGE 153

71. The North Halfmoon Lakes

ROUND-TRIP DISTANCE	8.2 miles
HIKING TIME	Up in 105 minutes, down in 77 minutes
STARTING ELEVATION	10,520 feet
HIGHEST ELEVATION	12,225 feet
ELEVATION GAIN	2,035 feet (includes an extra 165 feet each way)
DIFFICULTY	Moderate
MAPS	Trails Illustrated, Aspen/Independence Pass, Number 127 Mount Massive 7.5 minute Lake County San Isabel National Forest

COMMENT: The two North Halfmoon Lakes lie between a pair of Colorado's one hundred highest peaks: Mount Massive and Mount Oklahoma. Other nearby mountain giants, including Mount Elbert and French Mountain, hover above adjacent valleys. Both lakes are located above timberline in the Mount Massive Wilderness. The main trail up this valley proceeds to the north (right) of these lakes and eventually fades away, well above 12,000 feet. The major foot traffic in this basin consists of hikers on an alternate route up Mount Massive, Colorado's second highest summit.

GETTING THERE: From U.S. 24, near the southern edge of Leadville, drive west on Colorado 300 for 0.8 mile. Then turn left on Lake County Road 11 and set your mileage to zero. Go south on this road and turn right at mile 1.2, at the sign for Halfmoon Campground. Keep left at a fork at mile 2.6, eventually pass the Mount Elbert and Mount Massive trailheads, and cross Halfmoon Creek. The road becomes rougher. Stay on the main road and avoid a left fork at mile 9.5. Follow Road 110 for a rockier 0.5 mile and park on the right at the North Halfmoon trailhead signboard and register. Regular cars with high clearance can reach this trailhead. (Walking the last 0.5 mile on Road 110 is an alternative.)

THE HIKE: Start walking on the trail leading northwest from the trailhead. Quickly enter the wilderness area, pass through the forest and reach a large clearing after 1.3 miles from the trailhead. Mount Oklahoma comes into view at the head of the valley. After another mile, pass a cairn and a trail on the right leading toward Mount Massive. Continue up the main trail and soon pass two bare tree trunks on the left. 1 mile past these snags lies a key intersection at another rock pile. A faint trail will be seen leading north-

Lower and Upper Halfmoon Lakes.

PHOTO BY ALEX HUDGINS

northwest over North Halfmoon Creek, which is cascading down from the northwest. Mount Oklahoma will be located due west. Follow this side path off of the main trail and within 200 yards reach the lower North Halfmoon Lake with its clear, deep water. A faint trail leads north another 0.5 mile to reach the equally beautiful upper lake. Mount Oklahoma and the Continental Divide loom above to the left (west).

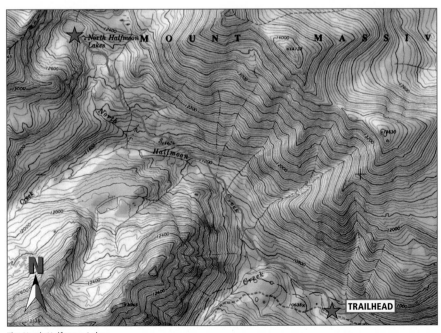

The North Halfmoon Lakes.

72. Lake Ann

ROUND-TRIP DISTANCE	12 miles
HIKING TIME	Up in 150 minutes, down in 122 minutes
STARTING ELEVATION	10,250 feet
HIGHEST ELEVATION	11,805 feet
ELEVATION GAIN	2,825 feet (includes 635 extra feet each way)
DIFFICULTY	More difficult
MAPS	Trails Illustrated, Buena Vista/Collegiate Peaks, Number 129 Winfield 7.5 minute Chaffee County Number 1 San Isabel National Forest

COMMENT: Lake Ann is located high in a remote basin of the Collegiate Peaks Wilderness, beneath the Continental Divide. Rocky peaks, many of them unnamed, ring the lake. Remnants of Colorado history abound along the route to Lake Ann. Driving to the trailhead, you pass by the former mining towns of Vicksburg, Rockdale, and Winfield. On the hiking trail you pass the former Banker Mine on the left and walk through an open area where the town of Hamilton once stood.

GETTING THERE: From the intersection with Colorado 82, south of Leadville, drive south on U.S. 24 for 4.2 miles and turn right onto Chaffee Road 390. Pass the Clear Creek Reservoir on the left and drive on this good, dirt road for 11.7 miles to the former town site of Winfield. Turn left at a fork, cross Clear Creek and, after 0.2 mile from Winfield, park on the right. (The road is blocked after 2 more miles. High clearance and four-wheel-drive are advised for this final 2 mile road segment.)

THE HIKE: Hike south from your parking area and at mile 1.5 pass the Banker Mine on the left and keep straight at a four-way intersection. Persist on the rough road another 0.5 mile to a trailhead sign and register, where the road is blocked. Continue on the road and, within 100 yards from the roadblock, reach a wilderness sign and a trail on the left at a sign. This footpath on the left leads to Huron Peak, a Fourteener. You continue straight on the South Fork Clear Creek Trail. At mile 2.9, pass a small wilderness sign. At mile 3.6, cross a meadow that was once occupied by the mining town of Hamilton. The formidable mountains known as The Three Apostles are visible on your left. Go right here at a signed fork. The left fork ascends to Apostle Basin. A

Lake Ann.

PHOTO BY BOB WATKINS

Continental Divide Trail symbol marks the right (south) fork, which you follow across a sturdy bridge over the South Fork of Clear Creek. Follow this good trail as it steepens for another mile to a crucial fork. The right fork is marked by another Continental Divide Trail symbol and the left fork is unmarked. Go left (south-southeast) on this adequate trail, which soon crosses the creek on three logs. In 1.4 miles the trail reaches circular Lake Ann at the far southern end of the basin, at timberline under the Continental Divide. If you lose the trail, follow the creek up to the lake. Huron Peak can be seen to the northeast and the rugged South Apostle to the east. Granite Peak is the closest mountain to the north-northwest. Enjoy and then retrace your ascent route back to the trailhead.

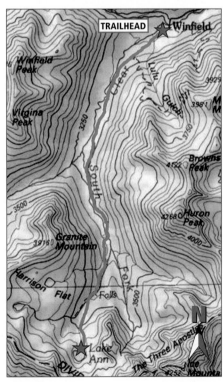

Lake Ann.

73. Deluge Lake

ROUND-TRIP DISTANCE	9 miles
HIKING TIME	Up in 155 minutes, down in 140 minutes
STARTING ELEVATION	8,690 feet
HIGHEST ELEVATION	11,760 feet
ELEVATION GAIN	4,190 feet (includes 560 extra feet each way)
DIFFICULTY	More difficult
MAPS	Trails Illustrated, Vail/Frisco/Dillon, Number 108 Vail East 7.5 minute Willow Lakes 7.5 minute Eagle County Numbers 2 and 4 White River National Forest

COMMENT: Considerable snow lingers in the higher tree-covered areas north of Interstate 70 and Vail until late July. Then you will be richly rewarded with the natural beauty of the steep, strenuous hike to Deluge Lake in the Eagles Nest Wilderness. Aspen trees abound and the wild flowers are everywhere in this lush area. Bikes are forbidden on the trail and dogs must be leashed.

GETTING THERE: From exit 180 off Interstate 70 east of Vail, drive east on the frontage road (The Bighorn Road), on the south side of the highway, for 2.2 miles and park off the road at the trailhead on the left.

THE HIKE: Start northeast past a signboard. Within 100 yards, take a left fork at a sign and continue west until the trail turns right and ascends steeply to the north-northeast. The trail may be overgrown and faint at times as you ascend past several talus and boulder fields on your left, and an occasional small creek crossing. Eventually you descend across a creek and enter the Deluge Creek drainage. Deluge Creek will be encountered after 3.6 miles from the trailhead, as the trail curves left (north). Cross the creek and follow the trail as it ascends north through a beautiful, extensive valley to reach Deluge Lake at the head of the creek, encircled by high, unnamed peaks. The lake is 0.9 mile above the initial encounter with Deluge Creek. Enjoy the setting with a great view down to the south of the Mount of the Holy Cross. Gather your forces for the lengthy descent and be careful to leave Deluge Creek and ascend south-southwest out of that drainage on the ascent trail.

Deluge Lake.

PHOTO BY DAVE COOPER

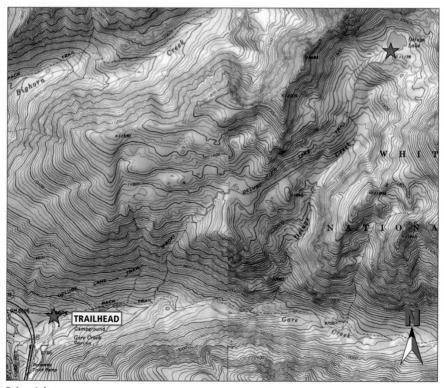

Deluge Lake.

74. Pitkin Lake

ROUND-TRIP DISTANCE	11 miles
HIKING TIME	Up in 160 minutes, down in 113 minutes
STARTING ELEVATION	8,390 feet
HIGHEST ELEVATION	11,380 feet
ELEVATION GAIN	3,520 feet (includes 265 extra feet each way)
DIFFICULTY	More difficult
MAPS	Trails Illustrated, Vail/Frisco/Dillon, Number 108 Vail East 7.5 minute Eagle County Number 2 White River National Forest

COMMENT: The hike to Pitkin Lake in the Eagles Nest Wilderness is one of the most scenic in the Vail area. The long and steep trail runs west of Pitkin Creek through vegetation to reach lovely Pitkin Lake, just below timberline, in a rocky bowl. The trail is clear throughout and passes through many aspen trees in the first half, with evergreens for the higher segments. The lake is named after Frederick Pitkin, who was governor of Colorado from 1879 to 1883.

GETTING THERE: Drive to exit 180 of Interstate 70 on the east side of Vail. Take the exit and drive east on the frontage road north of the highway. Follow this road for 500 feet and park on the left at the trailhead just after crossing over Pitkin Creek.

Climbers above Pitkin Lake. PHOTO BY DAVE COOPER

THE HIKE: Begin north from the trailhead signboard and register. Quickly cross Pitkin Creek and then ascend steeply. Within 1 mile the grade becomes more gradual. After 2.5 miles, Lower Pitkin Falls is visible to the right (east). Continue up through a series of rocky benches and lush meadows to finally reach Pitkin Lake at the head of the valley. The nearby peaks are part of the Gore Range. The imposing peak to the north-northwest is called the West Partner. The equally formidable mountain to the northeast is the East Partner. Both of these names are unofficial but are often used by mountain regulars. Watch your footing on the occasional gravel and loose rock on the steep return trip.

Pitkin Lake.

75. Grouse Lake

ROUND-TRIP DISTANCE	12.4 miles
HIKING TIME	Up in 162 minutes, down in 102 minutes
STARTING ELEVATION	7,820 feet
HIGHEST ELEVATION	10,700 feet
ELEVATION GAIN	3,330 feet (includes 225 extra feet each way)
DIFFICULTY	More difficult
MAPS	Trails Illustrated, Vail/Frisco/Dillon, Number 108 Minturn 7.5 minute Eagle County Number 4 White River National Forest

COMMENT: Isolated Grouse Lake experiences light hiking traffic and lies in the Holy Cross Wilderness west of Minturn. The route is lengthy, mostly shaded, and only especially scenic at Grouse Lake, at the foot of Grouse Mountain. The good trail crosses Grouse Creek several times. Due to the many crossings of flowing water, the latter half of the hiking season through the first week of October is the best time for this outing.

GETTING THERE: From Interstate 70 between Vail on the east and Avon on the west, take exit 171 at Dowds Junction. Drive south on U.S. 24 for 1.7 miles and park on the right, near a metal gate and the signboard for the Grouse Creek Trail.

THE HIKE: From the parking area and trailhead signboard, begin southeast on the Grouse Creek trail. The trail curves up to the right and within 50 yards passes a trail on the right, which leads to the Meadow Mountain Trail. Continue upward another 50 yards to a signed fork and go right. After 0.25 mile from this fork, go left (south-southwest) at a sign pole and fork. (The right fork ascends the West Grouse Creek drainage and leads to Olsen Lake, Grouse Mountain, and beyond.) After 0.5 mile up through the trees, take a right fork and make the first of a half dozen creek crossings. Continue then up the valley for over 5 more miles to reach Grouse Lake, with Grouse Mountain beyond to the southwest and a rocky ridge on the right (west). Enjoy the beautiful, peaceful setting before the long return. There are some views of the Gore Range to the north as you descend.

Grouse Lake with Grouse Mountain beyond.

PHOTO BY JOE ALDRIDGE

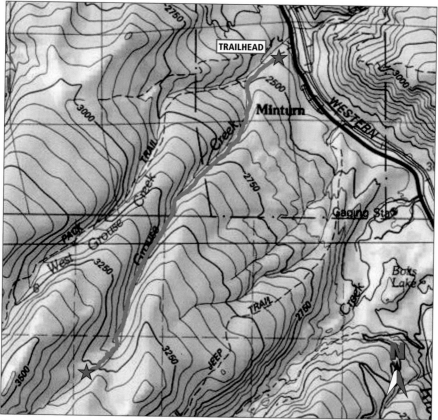

Grouse Lake.

76. Hunky Dory Lake

ROUND-TRIP DISTANCE	7 miles
HIKING TIME	Up in 95 minutes, down in 70 minutes
STARTING ELEVATION	9,320 feet
HIGHEST ELEVATION	11,300 feet
ELEVATION GAIN	2,090 feet (includes an extra 55 feet each way)
DIFFICULTY	Moderate
MAPS	Trails Illustrated, Holy Cross/Ruedi Reservoir, Number 126 Mount of the Holy Cross 7.5 minute Eagle County Number 4 White River National Forest

COMMENT: Hunky Dory Lake, located at the edge of the Holy Cross Wilderness, is a moderate destination in the midst of an area full of natural beauty and various hiking destinations. Holy Cross City, Cleveland Lake, Fancy Pass, and Fall Creek Pass can all be reached from the route to Hunky Dory Lake along French Creek.

GETTING THERE: From Interstate 70 west of Vail, take exit 171 and drive south on U.S. 24 through Minturn for 12.7 miles and turn right onto Homestake Road 703, which leads past the Blodgett Campground. This turnoff is also 9.7 miles north of Tennessee Pass on U.S. 24. Follow this good dirt road parallel to Homestake Creek for 7.3 miles. Park on the right at Gold Park, near a sign describing the four-wheel-drive road to Holy Cross City.

THE HIKE: Begin west from Gold Park up the very rough road that ascends the valley through aspen groves on the north side of French Creek. After 1.5 miles a road joins your road from the left. Continue up to the northwest. At 2.9 miles from the trailhead, pass a signboard, and cross Fancy Creek. Keep straight and pass around a vehicle barrier as a road leads left toward Holy Cross City and beyond. The final 0.5 mile takes you into more open terrain and Hunky Dory Lake on your left. Whitney Peak rises above to the north. The trail continues northwest and then north past the Seven Sisters Lakes and over Fall Creek Pass to Lake Constantine and the Fall Creek drainage. To return, retrace your ascent route.

Hunky Dory Lake.

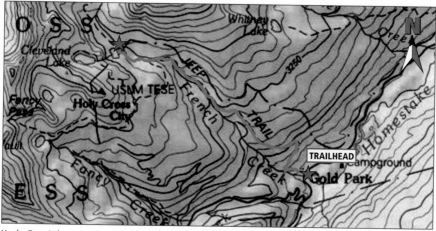

Hunky Dory Lake.

77. Lake Constantine

ROUND-TRIP DISTANCE	9.6 miles
HIKING TIME	Up in 115 minutes, down in 100 minutes
STARTING ELEVATION	10,320 feet
HIGHEST ELEVATION	11,417 feet
ELEVATION GAIN	1,927 feet (includes 415 extra feet each way)
DIFFICULTY	Moderate
MAPS	Trails Illustrated, Holy Cross/Ruedi Reservoir, Number 126 Minturn 7.5 minute Mount of the Holy Cross 7.5 minute Eagle County Number 4 White River National Forest

COMMENT: Most people who drive to the end of the Tigiwon Road are hikers who wish to climb the Mount of the Holy Cross. This will explain the many cars often parked around the trailhead. Your hike is more gradual and will pass by the trail to Notch Mountain. Flowers are abundant and there are good views to the east, down to the Fall Creek Valley.

GETTING THERE: From Interstate 70 west of Vail, take exit 171 and drive south on U.S. 24 for 5.0 miles and turn right onto the unpaved Tigiwon Road. Keep left at two early forks and stay on the main road for 8.1 miles from U.S. 24. At this point, the road ends at a parking area and two trailheads. Park here. The road is a bit rough but regular cars can reach the end.

Lake Constantine. 　　　　　　　　　　　PHOTO BY DAVE CALLAIS

Lake Constantine.

PHOTO BY DAVE CALLAIS

THE HIKE: Start to the east from the Fall Creek Trail sign. Avoid the trail to Halfmoon Pass. The trail is mostly shaded, but passes south through two steep, bare areas before reaching a sign and fork in 2.6 miles from the trailhead. (The right fork goes up to Notch Mountain.) You go left and in 2.2 more miles will pass over a bluff and descend to lovely Lake Constantine. Whitney Peak rises above to the south. The trail continues up over Fall Creek Pass and down to Hunky Dory Lake and beyond. Many people enjoy camping around Lake Constantine. Use the Fall Creek Trail again for your return.

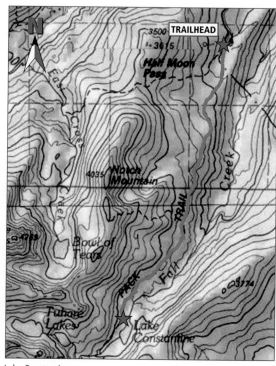

Lake Constantine.

169

78. Lonesome Lake

ROUND-TRIP DISTANCE	10.4 miles
HIKING TIME	Up in 134 minutes, down in 124 minutes
STARTING ELEVATION	10,140 feet
HIGHEST ELEVATION	11,550 feet
ELEVATION GAIN	2,470 feet (includes 530 extra feet each way)
DIFFICULTY	More difficult
MAPS	Trails Illustrated, Holy Cross/Ruedi Reservoir, Number 126 Homestake Reservoir 7.5 minute Eagle County Number 4 Pitkin County Number 2 White River National Forest

COMMENT: There are other Lonesome Lakes in Colorado. This one lies below the Continental Divide, west of Leadville, in the Holy Cross Wilderness. The route takes you up a lush alpine valley with the East Fork of Homestake Creek alongside the trail.

GETTING THERE: On U.S. 24, drive either 12.7 miles south from Interstate 70 or north 9.6 miles from Tennessee Pass and turn west onto Road 703. Follow this road past Blodgett Campground and go right at mile 6.7 from U.S. 24. Keep left at mile 7.7 and again at mile 10.2. At mile 10.5, just before Homestake Reservoir, park near a blocked road on the left. Regular cars can reach this point.

THE HIKE: From the parking area walk east up the blocked, steep four-wheel-drive road, with a large, functioning water pipe on your right. Continue up the road several hundred yards before the road ends and a trail begins through the trees, with the creek on your left.

Lonesome Lake.

PHOTO BY CLIF REED

Lonesome Lake.

PHOTO BY CLIF REED

The trail becomes faint at times, especially higher in the valley, but should be traceable. The trail rises and falls as it ascends toward timberline and the lake. There are several creek crossings. In the last 0.5 mile, as the trail becomes less clear, the open tundra can be full of flowers and very inviting. Pass a few ponds before reaching Lonesome Lake, which is cradled beneath the Continental Divide in a rocky cirque. There are many good sites for camping near the lake. Be careful to find the trail, in the higher areas especially, on your return. The Mount of the Holy Cross can be seen to the north, in the last 0.25 mile on the way back before you reach the trailhead.

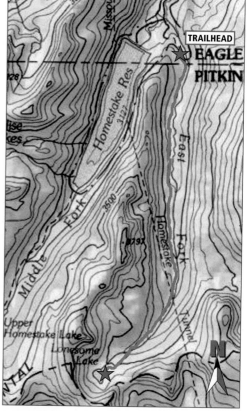

Lonesome Lake.

79. Eagle Lake

ROUND-TRIP DISTANCE	5.6 miles
HIKING TIME	Up in 70 minutes, down in 60 minutes
STARTING ELEVATION	9,380 feet
HIGHEST ELEVATION	10,077 feet
ELEVATION GAIN	1,217 feet (includes 260 extra feet each way)
DIFFICULTY	Moderate
MAPS	Trails Illustrated, Holy Cross/Ruedi Reservoir, Number 126 Crooked Creek Pass 7.5 minute Mount Jackson 7.5 minute Eagle County Numbers 3 and 4 White River National Forest

COMMENT: The rewards of the long drive from the Front Range to the Eagle Lake Trailhead (150 miles from Denver) include exposure to many out-of-the-way side roads and trails, passing by Sylvan Lake State Park (15.3 miles from U.S. 6), and a nice hike into the Holy Cross Wilderness to reach scenic Eagle Lake. Halfmoon Lake, Fairview Lake, and Strawberry Lake lie farther up the valley.

GETTING THERE: From Interstate 70, take exit 147 and drive south 0.3 mile to U.S. 6 and turn right to Eagle. Turn left quickly onto Broadway and after 0.3 mile more follow the Brush Creek Road signs to the left and then right after one block. Stay on the Brush Creek Road, which is paved for the first 10.6 miles from U.S. 6. Keep right at the fork at mile 10.6 and stay on the good dirt road another 10.1 miles to Crooked Creek Pass. Keep straight on the main road (National Forest Road 400) and descend 3.2 miles and take the left fork onto Road 507 at a sign. Follow this road 0.5 mile and take another left fork for 1.1 more miles to the trailhead on the left, just before the road is blocked. Regular cars can reach this point. (This trailhead can also be reached from Colorado 82 via Basalt and Thomasville, which is 9 miles south on Road 400 from the fork that leads to the Eagle Lake Trailhead.)

THE HIKE: Start hiking north on the good trail from the trailhead sign. Enter an aspen forest, pass through an unlocked gate, and follow the trail as it rises and falls past private property and Woods Lake on the right. After joining a dirt road, go east and soon pass an electric power shack on your left. Then cross Lime Creek, first on a bridge and then on a log. The trail then rises

Eagle Lake and Eagle Peak.

PHOTO BY DAVE MULLER

more steeply past some good overlooks of cascading Lime Creek. The creek will always be on your left until you reach the lovely lake, with a solitary tree in the water near its south shore. The trail ends here with Eagle Peak looming above to the northeast. The valley ascends further west to several more lakes and Avalanche Peak.

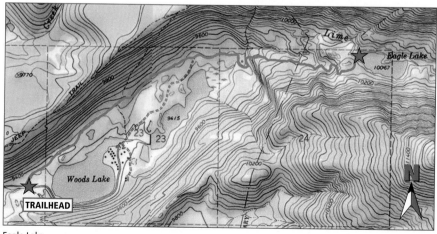

Eagle Lake.

80. Nolan Lake

ROUND-TRIP DISTANCE	7 miles
HIKING TIME	Up in 106 minutes, down in 82 minutes
STARTING ELEVATION	9,920 feet
HIGHEST ELEVATION	11,342 feet
ELEVATION GAIN	1,996 feet (includes 574 extra feet)
DIFFICULTY	Moderate
MAPS	Trails Illustrated, Eagle/Avon, Number 121, and Holy Cross/Ruedi Reservoir, Number 126 Fulford 7.5 minute Mount Jackson 7.5 minute Crooked Creek Pass 7.5 minute Eagle County Number 3 White River National Forest

COMMENT: How about a picnic at Nolan Lake beneath impressive Gold Dust Peak? This lovely hike is all it takes. Named after William Nolan, an early Fulford Prospector, the lake is reached by a good trail, which passes through the remnants of the upper town of Fulford. You will hike through several clearings before passing by a waterfall of Nolan Creek and then curving clockwise to ascend to the lake.

GETTING THERE: From Interstate 70, between Glenwood Springs and Vail, take exit 147 and drive south to Eagle. Then turn left onto Broadway in Eagle and follow the signs to Sylvan Lake. Once you get on the Brush Creek Road (which eventually crosses Crooked Creek Pass and descends to the Frying-pan Road, east of the Ruedi Reservoir), you will drive only 10.8 miles south from Eagle, still on the Brush Creek Road. Then turn left just before a bridge and follow the good, dirt road along East Brush Creek to Fulford. From the Brush Creek Road, stay on the main road, keep straight at mile 4.2, and again at mile 5.9. Take a left fork at mile 6.2, go right at mile 6.9, and left at mile 7.0. Go straight at mile 8.7 and reach a fork with Fulford on the left at mile 9.9. Nolan Creek passes under the road here and the trailhead for Nolan Lake is 30 feet ahead on the right. Park off road.

THE HIKE: Start walking southeast up the rough road, which is blocked to car traffic. A register lies on the left. After passing through the old upper town, the trail reaches a fork. A sign directs you up to the left. Go right at an ensuing fork at another sign. The trail meanders through lovely terrain,

Nolan Lake.

PHOTO BY JOE ALDRIDGE

passes some talus and boulders on the left and, later, the waterfall on the right. After entering the Holy Cross Wilderness, you reach a lovely meadow. Another sign directs you up a steeper segment to finally reach Nolan Lake, over a bluff, at 11,260 feet. The trail continues along the right side of the lake to the northwest to reach a larger boulder at the edge of the lake. This provides a great overlook back toward Fulford and beyond to the northwest. Gold Dust Peak looms above to the southeast, Craig Peak to the west, and New York Mountain to the north-northeast. Revel in the natural beauty and return as you ascended.

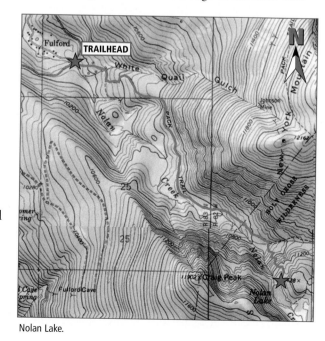

Nolan Lake.

81. Lake Charles and Mystic Island Lake

ROUND-TRIP DISTANCE	5.0 miles to Lake Charles, 1.2 miles further to Mystic Island Lake (Total 6.2 miles each way) 12.4 miles round-trip
HIKING TIME	Up to Lake Charles in 126 minutes, 35 minutes further to Mystic Island Lake, down in 133 minutes
STARTING ELEVATION	9,435 feet
HIGHEST ELEVATION	11,300 feet
ELEVATION GAIN	3,955 feet (includes 2,090 extra feet)
DIFFICULTY	More difficult
MAPS	Trails Illustrated, Holy Cross/Ruedi Reservoir, Number 126 Crooked Creek Pass 7.5 minute Mount Jackson 7.5 minute Eagle County Numbers 3 and 4 White River National Forest

COMMENT: Deep in the Holy Cross Wilderness, Lake Charles and Mystic Island Lake provide beautiful hike destinations. They lie at the head of a rocky basin surrounded by three majestic peaks. The long trail is adequate but obscure at certain brief segments. Brush Creek is always on your right as you ascend.

GETTING THERE: From Interstate 70, between Vail and Glenwood Springs, take exit 147 and drive through the town of Eagle. Go left after 0.5 mile from Interstate 70 and follow the signs to Sylvan Lake and reach the Brush Creek Road. (This paved road proceeds south and eventually crosses Crooked Creek Pass and descends to the Fryingpan Road, east of the Ruedi Reservoir and Basalt.) At mile 10.9 from Interstate 70, take the unpaved road on the left, at a sign just before the main road crosses Brush Creek on a bridge. Follow this good dirt road and keep right at mile 4.2, left at mile 5.8, and right at mile 6.2 from the paved Brush Creek Road. At mile 7.2, reach the Fulford Cave Campground and go left at a fork. Park at road end and a trailhead sign at mile 7.3. Regular cars can reach this point.

THE HIKE: From the trailhead sign, begin east and within thirty yards go left at a signed fork. (The right fork is the Iron Edge Trail, which is used for horse traffic and provides a longer route to Lake Charles.) Continue up and enter the trees. After 1 mile from the trailhead, pass a pond on the left and proceed to the southeast. Higher in the basin you pass by some striking rocky cliffs and occasionally cross side creeks descending from your left. Finally, reach Lake Charles and enjoy this pristine body of water. Continue

Lake Charles.

PHOTO BY JOE ALDRIDGE

by trail to the east with Lake Charles on your right. It is another 1.2 miles through some open marshy terrain to Mystic Island Lake at the end of the valley. A small island, on the far right side of the lake, gives it its name. Eagle Peak lies ahead to the southeast.

Fools Peak hovers above to the south-southwest and Gold Dust Peak can be seen to the north. Enjoy the fruits of your laborious hike before the long trek back to the trailhead.

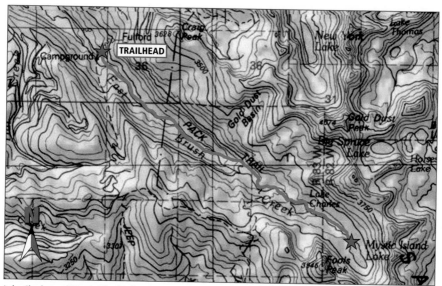

Lake Charles and Mystic Island Lake.

82. Lost Man Reservoir

ROUND-TRIP DISTANCE	1 mile
HIKING TIME	Up in 13 minutes, down in 13 minutes
STARTING ELEVATION	10,504 feet
HIGHEST ELEVATION	10,580 feet
ELEVATION GAIN	256 feet (includes 90 extra feet each way)
DIFFICULTY	Easy
MAPS	Trails Illustrated, Aspen/Independence Pass, Number 127 Mt. Champion 7.5 minute Pitkin County Number 2 White River National Forest

COMMENT: A short hike to an isolated body of water, such as Lost Man Reservoir, can make a wonderful family outing. Young and old can experience the natural beauty of the high country. Trails to both Midway Pass and South Fork Pass lie nearby for the hiker desiring more challenge. Lost Man Creek runs into this reservoir, which then empties into the Roaring Fork River, which courses into Aspen.

GETTING THERE: On U.S. 82 between Aspen and Independence Pass, drive either 11.4 miles northwest from Independence Pass or 8.2 miles southeast from Mill Street and Main Street (which is Colorado 82) in central Aspen. Park off the south side of the road at a turnoff area.

Lost Man Reservoir.　　　　　　　　　　　　PHOTO BY JUDY HERZANEK

Lost Man Reservoir from above with the Geissler Mountains beyond.

PHOTO BY JUDY HERZANEK

THE HIKE: From the trailhead signboard, begin on the trail leading to the west. Quickly cross a sturdy bridge and within a few hundred yards keep left (north) at an unmarked trail fork. After another fifty yards, you will reach a sign and trail junction. The left trail leads southwest toward Midway Pass. You proceed, however, to the right (north-northeast) on the Lost Man Trail, which curls up to the dam and Lost Man Reservoir on the right. The trail continues northward up the valley. The Geissler Mountains hover across the reservoir. Take it all in before retracing your route back to the trailhead.

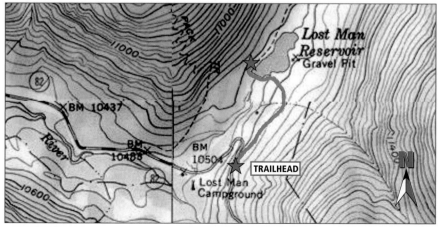

Lost Man Reservoir.

83. Linkins Lake

ROUND-TRIP DISTANCE	1.6 miles
HIKING TIME	Up in 21 minutes, down in 19 minutes
STARTING ELEVATION	11,506 feet
HIGHEST ELEVATION	12,008 feet
ELEVATION GAIN	542 feet (includes 20 extra feet each way)
DIFFICULTY	Easy
MAPS	Trails Illustrated, Aspen/Independence Pass, Number 127
	Independence Pass 7.5 minute
	Mount Champion 7.5 minute
	Pitkin County Number 2
	White River National Forest

COMMENT: It is unusual to access a high mountain lake, like Linkins Lake, so easily. With a starting point just below timberline, you can reach the lake in less than 1 mile. Being above the trees affords the hiker great vistas. Other destinations in this basin are the higher Independence Lake and Geissler Mountain, with its east and west summits.

GETTING THERE: From Independence Pass on Colorado 82, drive west for 1.8 miles and park on the north side of the road as it curves sharply to the left. This point can also be reached by driving 17.9 miles on Colorado 82, east from the center of Aspen at Mill and Main Streets.

THE HIKE: The hike begins to the northwest, past a trail sign and register. After 0.25 mile, cross a small creek and go left at a fork and a sign indicating that you are entering the Hunter-Fryingpan Wilderness. (The Fryingpan River originates in this basin.) Follow the main trail up through the rocky, treeless terrain. Occasional side trails may confuse you. Your destination is the grassy bench above, to the northwest. Upon reaching this bench, it is less than 0.1 mile over the tundra to the peaceful shores of large Linkins Lake. North and northwest, respectively, are East and West Geissler Mountains. Twining Peak is the high peak to the east-northeast. Be careful on the steep parts of the trail during your short return to the parking area.

SIDEBAR: Independence Pass

Careful. On the Aspen side of Independence Pass the paved road, while passable, is a tad bit narrow and might be considered "sporty" by the unitiated.

Linkins Lake.

PHOTO BY DAVE MULLER

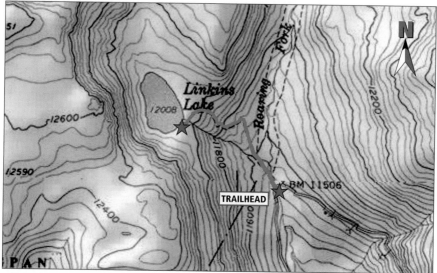

Linkins Lake.

84. Cathedral Lake

ROUND-TRIP DISTANCE	7 miles
HIKING TIME	Up in 90 minutes, down in 60 minutes
STARTING ELEVATION	9,880 feet
HIGHEST ELEVATION	11,910 feet
ELEVATION GAIN	2,470 feet (includes 440 extra feet)
DIFFICULTY	Moderate
MAPS	Trails Illustrated, Aspen/Independence Pass, Number 127 Hayden Peak 7.5 minute Pitkin County Number 2 White River National Forest

COMMENT: The hike to Cathedral Lake in the Maroon Bells–Snowmass Wilderness is one of the grandest in Colorado. Thick groves of aspen, the rushing waters of Pine Creek, and thrilling vistas reward the hiker before reaching this large, gorgeous lake, lying in a rocky bowl beneath two of Colorado's highest peaks.

GETTING THERE: From Colorado 82, 0.5 mile west of the Castle Creek Bridge, turn south. Within 30 yards, go left on the Castle Creek Road. Follow the paved road up this lovely valley through Ashcroft, for a total of 11.9 miles from Colorado 82. Turn right onto a dirt road with a sign giving the distance to Cathedral Lake and the trailhead parking area. Follow this road for 0.6 mile and park near the trailhead at road end. Regular cars can reach this trailhead.

Cathedral Lake.   PHOTO BY DAVE COOPER

Ginni Greer looking down on Cathedral Lake.

PHOTO BY DAVE COOPER

THE HIKE: Your trek begins to the south-southwest from the trailhead sign and register. Follow the good trail through a thick aspen grove. Soon the waters of Pine Creek, descending from Cathedral Lake, appear on your left. Pass through several fields of talus and boulders and eventually ascend a series of switchbacks that take you up through a talus slope to enter the forest on a shelf trail. Then quickly reach a signed fork at mile 2.8 from the trailhead. Descend the left fork. (The trail on the right ascends to Electric Pass.) You will soon reach another signed fork. Stay to the left again and cross Pine Creek. (The right fork again leads to Electric Pass.) Then ascend gently to a grassy bench overlooking the lake. Follow either of two trails down to Cathedral Lake and savor the beauty all around you before your return. Cathedral Peak is the rocky behemoth to the west-northwest. Conundrum Peak rises above to the south, and over your shoulder to the northwest is Electric Pass Peak.

SEE MAP PAGE 185

183

85. American Lake

ROUND-TRIP DISTANCE	6.8 miles
HIKING TIME	Up in 115 minutes, down in 76 minutes
STARTING ELEVATION	9,400 feet
HIGHEST ELEVATION	11,372 feet
ELEVATION GAIN	2,132 feet (includes an extra 80 feet each way)
DIFFICULTY	Moderate
MAPS	Trails Illustrated, Aspen/Independence Pass, Number 127 Hayden Peak 7.5 minute Pitkin County Number 2 White River National Forest

COMMENT: The hikes to both American Lake and its southern neighbor, Cathedral Lake, in the Maroon Bells–Snowmass Wilderness, are especially scenic. The route to American Lake is steep at times and uses many switch-backs as it passes through lovely forest. From the lake, which empties into Devaney Creek, Leahy Peak can be seen to the south.

GETTING THERE: From the middle of Aspen, at Main Street and East Mill Street, drive west on Colorado 82 for 1.3 miles and turn left onto the road to both Ashcroft and the Maroon Bells. Within 30 yards of this turn, go left at a fork and follow the paved Castle Creek Road for 9.8 miles and turn right into the American Lake trailhead and parking.

American Lake. PHOTO BY DAVE COOPER

American Lake from above.

THE HIKE: Begin west from the trail sign. Cross a meadow and in 200 yards keep left. The trail rises through the trees with occasional switchbacks. After 1.0 mile keep left (south-southwest) at a four-way trail intersection. After crossing an area of fallen timber, traverse some lovely clearings and two talus slopes before reaching small American Lake. This lake is in a bowl near timberline, beneath rocky slopes to the west. Return as you ascended.

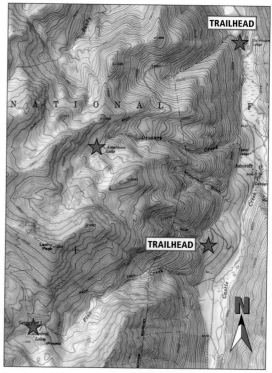

American Lake (upper center). Cathedral Lake (lower left).

185

86. Williams Lake

ROUND-TRIP DISTANCE	6.6 miles
HIKING TIME	Up in 88 minutes, down in 80 minutes
STARTING ELEVATION	9,430 feet
HIGHEST ELEVATION	10,815 feet
ELEVATION GAIN	1,585 feet (includes an extra 100 feet each way)
DIFFICULTY	Moderate
MAPS	Trails Illustrated, Maroon Bells/Redstone/Marble, Number 128 Capitol Peak 7.5 minute Pitkin County Number 1 White River National Forest

COMMENT: The trailhead for Williams Lake is adjacent to the Capitol Peak trailhead. From your parking area, impressive Mount Daly and Capitol Peak can be seen across the valley to the south. Most of the cars parked in this area will be those of Capitol Peak hikers. (Your access road continues further southwest beyond where you parked, for another 0.8 mile to end at a trailhead sign, but four-wheel-drive would be necessary.)

GETTING THERE: Drive on Colorado 82 either north from the Castle Creek Bridge in Aspen for 13.8 miles or south from Glenwood Springs for 23 miles. At the Snowmass Post Office, on the south side of the highway, turn south onto the Snowmass Creek Road and drive for 1.8 miles to a T. Turn right and drive southwest on the Capitol Creek Road. After 4.9 miles from the T, the road paving ends. Continue on the dirt road for 3.4 more miles to an open area. Park around here. The road is quite rough for the last mile but regular cars with high clearance will be able to come this far.

Williams Lake. PHOTO BY FRANK BURZYNSKI

The clear waters of Williams Lake.

PHOTO BY FRANK BURZYNSKI

THE HIKE: Start west on the steep road through an aspen grove and in 0.6 mile reach a fork. The trail on the left and the road to the right will reconvene 0.2 mile further, at a trail signboard for Hell Roaring Trail, Number 1960. Continue south-southwest around a gate and past a Maroon Bells–Snowmass Wilderness sign. In 0.3 mile from the road end you will reach a fork and continue straight. (The right fork leads quickly to Hardscrabble Lake.) After 0.5 mile from this fork you will reach another. Turn right at the sign for Williams Lake. Descend slightly, cross a creek and then ascend up to beautiful Williams Lake. On your way back a side trip to Hardscrabble Lake will require a total of less than ten minutes extra hiking time.

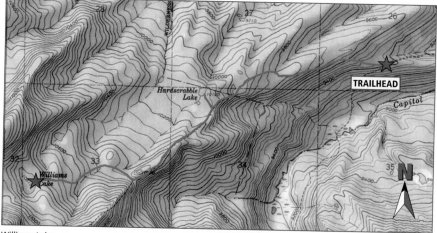

Williams Lake.

87. Chapman Lake

ROUND-TRIP DISTANCE	1.8 miles
HIKING TIME	Up in 22 minutes, down in 19 minutes
STARTING ELEVATION	9,600 feet
HIGHEST ELEVATION	9,790 feet
ELEVATION GAIN	400 feet (includes 105 extra feet each way)
DIFFICULTY	Easy
MAPS	Trails Illustrated, Holy Cross/Ruedi Reservoir, Number 126 Meredith 7.5 minute Pitkin County Number 2 White River National Forest

COMMENT: A gentle, short hike to a lovely lake in a remote area can be enjoyable and refreshing for hikers of all ages and abilities. One such outing leads to lovely Chapman Lake, east of Basalt and the Ruedi Reservoir. The trail is good, with a few steeper areas as it passes through the woods in the Hunter-Fryingpan Wilderness. Bicycles are forbidden.

GETTING THERE: From Colorado 82, drive east through the town of Basalt and up the Fryingpan Road, past the Ruedi Reservoir and the towns of Meredith and Thomasville, for a total of 27.7 miles. Turn right off the paved road at a sign for the Norrie Colony. Go straight, cross the creek, and after 200 yards, take a left fork and follow the good, wide dirt road as it curves up to the left. Keep left at mile 3.3 from the Fryingpan road at a sign, and right at mile 4.3 at another sign. At mile 4.9, park on the left at the trailhead. Regular cars can reach this point.

THE HIKE: Begin north on foot from the trailhead sign and register. Gradually ascend for 0.5 mile before the trail curves down to the right. Soon you will reach Chapman Lake on your right. Numerous water lilies are often present on the lake and two unnamed peaks can be seen across the lake to the south and to the south-southwest. It is a beautiful and tranquil scene if the weather is right. Enjoy it all before the easy return to your car at the trailhead.

SIDEBAR: Norrie Colony
Norrie Colony, now a residential area, was a railroad camp in the 19th century that was a logging operation to provide timbers for railroad construction.

Chapman Lake.

PHOTO BY FRANK BURZYNSKI

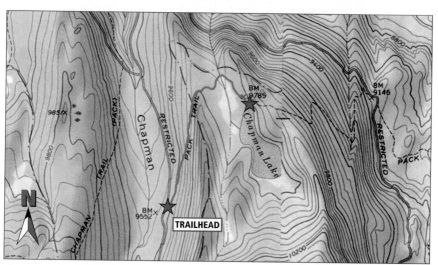

Chapman Lake.

88. Lower and Upper Savage Lakes

ROUND-TRIP DISTANCE	2.0 miles to Lower Savage Lake, 0.5 mile further to Upper Savage Lake (Total 5 miles round trip.)
HIKING TIME	Up to Lower Savage Lake in 50 minutes, 12 more minutes to Upper Savage Lake, down in 46 minutes from Upper Savage Lake (Total 108 minutes)
STARTING ELEVATION	9,880 feet
HIGHEST ELEVATION	11,140 feet
ELEVATION GAIN	1,660 feet (includes 200 extra feet each way)
DIFFICULTY	Moderate
MAPS	Trails Illustrated, Holy Cross/Ruedi Reservoir, Number 126 Nast 7.5 minute Eagle County Number 4 White River National Forest

COMMENT: The trail to both Savage Lakes is remote from population centers and experiences low usage. Lying in the Holy Cross Wilderness, the good, sometimes steep and rocky, trail follows a clockwise direction to the lakes, which are quite pretty and distinct. Good camping areas abound near both lakes and the terrain above to the east allows gradual access to the ridge, with Savage Peak to the left.

GETTING THERE: From Colorado 82 at Basalt, drive east on the Fryingpan Road for 26.2 miles. (En route to this point you pass by the Ruedi Reservoir, Meredith, and Thomasville.) Turn left and leave the paved road just before a bridge across the North Fork of the Fryingpan River. Take an immediate right fork and follow the good, wide, dirt road with the North Fork on your right. Continue on the main road, pass the Elk Wallow Campground at mile 3.0 from the Fryingpan Road and go left at an unmarked fork at mile 4.4. After 3.4 more miles, park on the right with the trailhead on the left and a creek alongside it to the east. Regular cars can reach this point.

THE HIKE: This hike begins north from the trailhead signboard and ascends through the forest, with the outflow creek from the two lakes always on your right. The trail is often steep and rocky. At mile 1.3 pass rocky cliffs, boulders, and talus on your left. Just before the lake, at a level area, there are several connecting trails. Generally persist in a southerly direction and quickly reach Lower Savage Lake, with a huge boulder at its northern edge. Continue on a faint trail around the lake to the left. Keep close to the edge of

Lower Savage Lake.

PHOTO BY CAMERON WENZEL

the lake until you reach a boulderfield, just before the inflow creek enters the lake at its southern end. Easily cross the boulders and take the trail ascending south. Keep the creek on your right; it is less than 100 feet of elevation gain until you reach Upper Savage Lake in the rocky bowl. Let the peace of this setting permeate you before returning by your ascent route. Savage Peak can be seen to the north-northwest from the southern end of Lower Savage Lake.

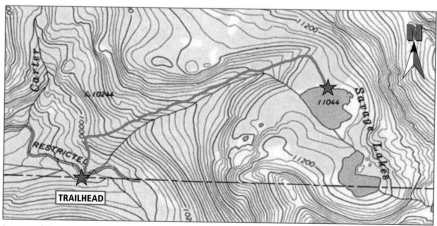

Lower and Upper Savage Lakes.

89. Lyle Lake and Mormon Lake

ROUND-TRIP DISTANCE	1.5 miles to Lyle Lake, another 1.8 miles to Mormon Lake (Total 6.6 miles round trip)
HIKING TIME	Up to Lyle Lake in 40 minutes, then to Mormon Lake in 55 minutes, return in 75 minutes (Total 170 minutes)
STARTING ELEVATION	10,720 feet
HIGHEST ELEVATION	11,680 feet
ELEVATION GAIN	1,670 feet (includes 710 extra feet)
DIFFICULTY	Moderate
MAPS	Trails Illustrated, Holy Cross/Ruedi Reservoir, Number 126 Nast 7.5 minute Pitkin County Number 2 White River National Forest

COMMENT: Lyle and Mormon Lakes are located in a remote area of the Holy Cross Wilderness. Their beauty and the surrounding grandeur easily make them worthwhile hiking targets. Lyle Lake is the larger and lies at the head of an open valley. Mormon Lake is more remote and requires passing through some rocky terrain. Camping and fishing around either lake could be delightful.

GETTING THERE: These lakes are reached from the Hagerman Pass Road. The easiest vehicular access is from the west. Drive east from Colorado 82 (between Glenwood Springs and Aspen) through Basalt and past the Ruedi Reservoir. Get on Road 105 and, from a signed fork (with the left road leading to Diemer Lake and Sellar Lake) drive the right fork, which is Road 105, the Hagerman Pass Road, for 7.4 more miles to a four-way intersection. The right fork leads to Ivanhoe Lake. Road 105 continues straight and becomes rougher. In another 0.1 mile, the trailhead and a small parking area lay on the left. (Access from the east requires a four-wheel-drive vehicle with high clearance. The trailhead lies 3.8 miles west of Hagerman Pass.) From the west, regular cars can reach the four-way intersection just before the trailhead.

THE HIKE: Begin northeast from the trailhead sign and register. Ascend gradually through mostly open meadow for 1.5 mile to scenic Lyle Lake. The rounded, grassy summit of Lyle Peak can be seen to the southeast. A faint trail surrounds the lake. The western side is grassy and the eastern side is rocky. Continue to the far end of the lake and ascend a steeper trail to the

Mormon Lake.

north-northeast. After reaching the high point of this hike, you will gradually descend by trail and occasional cairns. The trail passes below cliffs and boulders on the right and then briefly enters the trees. The final segment before Mormon Lake passes through lovely open tundra and alongside a small pond before a gentle descent to the north-northeast. The trail gets faint and ends near the lake. A rocky wall lies behind Mormon Lake, with gentler slopes above to the right. Return as you came. Use your compass and don't lose the trail.

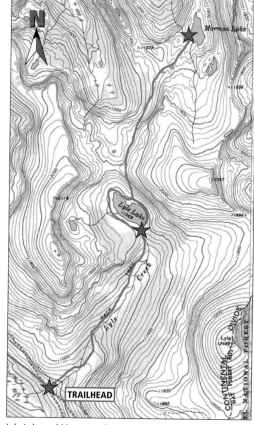

Lyle Lake and Mormon Lake.

90. The Thomas Lakes

ROUND-TRIP DISTANCE	7 miles
HIKING TIME	Up in 100 minutes, down in 80 minutes
STARTING ELEVATION	8,540 feet
HIGHEST ELEVATION	10,270 feet
ELEVATION GAIN	2,080 feet (includes 175 extra feet each way)
DIFFICULTY	Moderate
MAPS	Trails Illustrated, Maroon Bells/Redstone/Marble, Number 128 Basalt 7.5 minute Mount Sopris 7.5 minute Pitkin County Number 1 White River National Forest

COMMENT: Lying at the foot of imposing Mount Sopris and its high twin summits, the Thomas Lakes are a scenic hiking target. The two lakes lie within the Maroon Bells–Snowmass Wilderness, southwest of Glenwood Springs and Carbondale. The trail is lined by many aspen trees before the lakes and continues beyond to the top of Mount Sopris.

GETTING THERE: From Colorado 82, 1.6 miles northwest of the exit to Basalt, turn left (west), and quickly left again on the Emma Road. After 0.1 mile, turn right onto the Sopris Creek Road. After 1.2 miles from Colorado 82, reach a T and set your mileage to zero. Turn right onto the West Sopris Creek Road and, after 5.2 miles, turn right at a sign directing you to Dinkle Lake. Ascend 0.3 mile and pass a parking area on your right. Continue to the left another 0.1 mile to a fork and sign. Go left here for 2.0 more miles and park on the left opposite the trailhead, just before reaching Dinkle Lake. The final 2 miles are bumpy but regular cars can readily reach this trailhead parking area.

THE HIKE: Your walk begins to the south, past a signboard and register. Quickly turn left and ascend more steeply before the trail turns to the right. The wide trail is an old farming road. After 1.25 miles from the trailhead, leave the road and ascend a steep, narrow trail on the right. This trail leads to a treeless bench and great views of Mount Sopris. Follow the trail, which is a road again, into the trees to the south-southwest. Eventually make a steep ascent through an open area before the trail becomes more gradual

One of the Thomas Lakes and aspen gold.

PHOTO BY PENELOPE PURDY

over the final 0.3 mile. Pass a small, unnamed lake on the right before reaching the larger, lower Thomas Lake on the right. The upper lake lies 300 yards further to the left of the trail, which continues up to the ridge and eventually reaches the dual summits of Mount Sopris. It is noteworthy that both high points are of equal height. Enjoy the beauty and serenity of these two large lakes before returning by your ascent route.

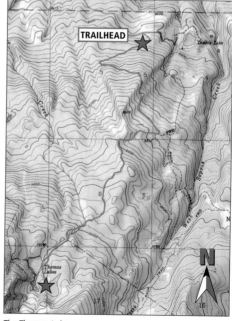

The Thomas Lakes.

91. Green Lake (Crested Butte)

ROUND-TRIP DISTANCE	9 miles
HIKING TIME	Up in 119 minutes, down in 104 minutes
STARTING ELEVATION	8,930 feet
HIGHEST ELEVATION	10,613 feet
ELEVATION GAIN	2,193 feet (includes 255 extra feet each way)
DIFFICULTY	Moderate
MAPS	Trails Illustrated, Crested Butte/Pearl Pass, Number 131, and Kebler Pass/Paonia Reservoir, Number 133 Crested Butte 7.5 minute Mount Axtell 7.5 minute Gunnison County Number 2 Gunnison Basin Area

COMMENT: Here is a hike which begins within the town of Crested Butte and ascends to lovely Green Lake at the foot of Mount Axtell. Laid out and well marked by the town of Crested Butte, the trail is open to hikers and bicyclists. Dogs must be kept on leash.

GETTING THERE: Drive to the southern end of Second Street in Crested Butte. Trailhead parking lies 50 yards south of Whiterock Avenue, opposite the Headwaters Nature Center.

THE HIKE: Start walking up a blocked road to the east-southeast. Within 0.2 mile, turn right on Journey's End Road. Pass several elegant homes. Just past a pond on the left, a sign leads you off of the road into the dense forest. The trail generally ascends to the west through thick forest to reach an old dirt road. Ascend left on this steep road for several hundred yards until a trail leaves the road to the right (southwest). After a brief walk through the trees, you reach the Wildcat Road. Follow this road to the right for 0.3 mile before leaving the road to the left (west) at a trail sign. You now ascend through a more lush forest. Eventually, Mount Axtell comes into view ahead. Continue up through a clearing and proceed straight at a four-way trail intersection. The trail soon descends slightly, crosses Wildcat Creek, passes a talus field on the left, and rises to aptly named Green Lake. The slopes of Mount Axtell invite the hiker who wants more. A bluff above the lake on the left provides views back toward Crested Butte. Your return on the ascent route will be easier and quicker.

From Green Lake down the valley.

PHOTO BY MARIA SMITH

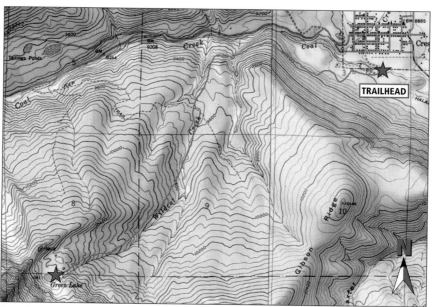

Green Lake.

92. Lost Lake (Gunnison County) and Dollar Lake

ROUND-TRIP DISTANCE	3 miles (total loop): 0.8 miles to Lost Lake, 0.9 miles over to Dollar Lake, down in 1.3 miles.
HIKING TIME	Up to Lost Lake in 21 minutes, over to Dollar Lake in 21 minutes, down in 34 minutes
STARTING ELEVATION	9,630 feet
HIGHEST ELEVATION	10,030 feet
ELEVATION GAIN	775 feet (includes 375 extra feet)
DIFFICULTY	Easy
MAPS	Trails Illustrated, Kebler Pass/Paonia Reservoir, Number 133 Anthracite Range 7.5 minute Gunnison County Number 2 Gunnison Basin Area – Gunnison National Forest

COMMENT: Here is a good, easy hike located west of Crested Butte, off of the Kebler Pass Road, for walkers of all ages. Three lakes are connected by a trail below East Beckwith Mountain. They are: Lost Lake Slough, Lost Lake, and Dollar Lake. A slough is defined as a marshy or swamp-like pool. The Lost Lake Slough is, however, to all appearances, a regular, scenic lake.

GETTING THERE: From Colorado 135 in Crested Butte, drive west on Whiterock Avenue, which becomes Gunnison Road Number 12, for 7.5 miles to Kebler Pass. Continue west on this good dirt road another 9.0 miles and turn left onto Road 706, which leads to the Lost Lake Campground and Lost Lake Slough in 2.5 miles. Park at the western end of the campground, at the edge of Lost Lake Slough, near the trailhead sign. Regular cars can easily reach this point.

THE HIKE: Begin to the south from the trailhead sign and soon enter the trees as you begin a counterclockwise loop. After 0.25 mile, you will cross a rough road. Follow the trail as it curves left and parallel to the road for 100 yards until road and trail unite. Soon Lost Lake emerges with a sign at its outlet. Continue east to Dollar Lake. A spur trail to the right after 0.3 mile leads quickly to a series of small waterfalls. Resume hiking to the east and reach a signed fork. Go right to reach round Dollar Lake after crossing a ridge.

Return to the fork and proceed down to the right to Lost Lake Slough and the campground road leading back to the trailhead.

From the edge of Lost Lake in Gunnison County.

PHOTO BY MARIA SMITH

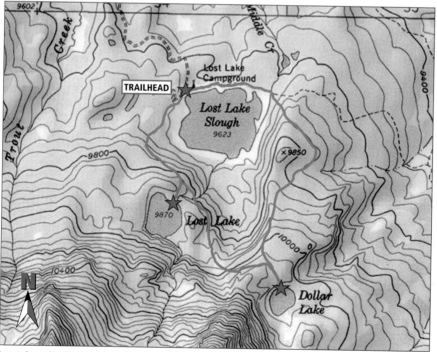

Lost Lake and Dollar Lake.

93. Copper Lake

ROUND-TRIP DISTANCE	9.4 miles
HIKING TIME	Up in 120 minutes, down in 100 minutes
STARTING ELEVATION	9,840 feet
HIGHEST ELEVATION	11,363 feet
ELEVATION GAIN	2,198 feet (includes 675 extra feet)
DIFFICULTY	Moderate
MAPS	Trails Illustrated, Maroon Bells/Redstone/Marble, Number 128, and Crested Butte/Pearl Pass, Number 131 Gothic 7.5 minute Maroon Bells 7.5 minute Gunnison County Number 2 Gunnison Basin Area – Gunnison National Forest

COMMENT: Copper Lake is on my top ten list for beautiful lakes in Colorado. Lying beneath East Maroon Pass and impressive peaks in the Maroon Bells–Snowmass Wilderness, the kidney-shaped lake is a high mountain jewel.

The route begins north of the town of Gothic and passes by Judd Falls as it continues up the valley, parallel to Copper Creek. There are three crossings of Copper Creek, and only one is made easier by a fallen log. If you don't like wading in cold mountain currents, save this hike for late August or September. Due to lingering snow high in the basin, I recommend this hike after the middle of July, at least.

GETTING THERE: From Elk Avenue in Crested Butte, drive north 7.8 miles on Gunnison Road 317, through Mount Crested Butte, and on the Gothic Road to the town of Gothic. From the town hall and visitor center in Gothic, continue north on the adequate dirt road for 0.6 mile and turn right at a fork. Follow this rough road another 0.5 mile to a parking area at the trailhead. The road is blocked at the trailhead. Regular cars can reach this parking area.

THE HIKE: From the parking area, hike east up a blocked road. There are good views of Mount Crested Butte and Gothic Mountain during the early part of the hike. Lose some elevation and arrive at a view of Judd Falls and a T intersection after 0.6 mile. Ascend to the left, past a trail register and signboard, and reach the first crossing of Copper Creek at mile 1.8. If you need an assist, a fallen tree trunk provides transit 10 yards above the wide trail. Avoid the narrow trail to the left just before the creek. Continue up the

Copper Lake from the East Maroon Pass Trail with Gothic Mountain beyond.

PHOTO BY RYAN LEWANDOWSKI

wide road, pass a talus slope on the right and reach the second Copper Creek crossing at mile 3.2 from the trailhead. Wade across here and again over a side creek a few hundred yards up the trail. Then wade across Copper Creek for the final time on your ascent at mile 3.5. Keep right at a fork just past the creek as the trail steepens. The left fork ascends to the Sylvanite Mine. It is 0.7 mile farther to a signed fork. The right fork leads to Triangle Pass and the Conundrum Creek Trail. You ascend steeply straight ahead and reach a map sign after another 0.25 mile. The sign clarifies camping sites and the East Maroon Pass Trail, which leads to the right. You go left (north-northwest) the final 0.25 mile and walk down to this gorgeous lake. The East Maroon Pass Trail can be seen ascending above the lake. Relax and enjoy this great setting. Maybe you would like to camp and fish before you return down the valley.

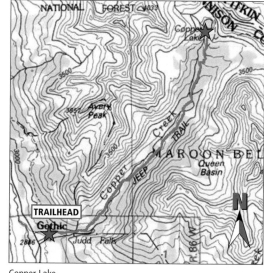

Copper Lake.

94. Mill Lake

ROUND-TRIP DISTANCE	5 miles
HIKING TIME	Up in 75 minutes, down in 50 minutes
STARTING ELEVATION	10,030 feet
HIGHEST ELEVATION	11,470 feet
ELEVATION GAIN	1,540 feet (includes 50 extra feet each way)
DIFFICULTY	Moderate
MAPS	Trails Illustrated, Gunnison/Pitkin, Number 132 Fairview Peak 7.5 minute Gunnison County Number 5 Gunnison Basin Area – Gunnison National Forest

COMMENT: The relatively short upward trek to Mill Lake in the Fossil Ridge Wilderness rewards the hiker with a serene, green lake beneath Fossil Mountain. Bicycles and all motorized vehicles are forbidden in the wilderness areas.

GETTING THERE: On U.S. 50, east of Gunnison, drive to Parlin and turn north on Gunnison Road 76, which leads to Ohio City. After 7.5 miles on this road, turn left at Ohio City onto Road 771 and follow it for 6.7 miles, near to the Gold Creek Campground, and park on the left near the trailhead sign. Regular cars can readily reach this point.

THE HIKE: From the sign at the trailhead, walk up to the north-northwest, through an open meadow and into the trees. After 0.4 mile, take the right fork to Mill Lake at signs and a trail register. (The left fork takes you on the Fossil Ridge Trail to Boulder Lake and beyond.) By ascending the trail on the right, you will enter the Fossil Ridge Wilderness. It is a little over 2 miles from here to Mill Lake. En route you cross two creeks and pass through a clearing full of fallen timber, about 1 mile below the lake. Follow the good trail with its many switchbacks until it ends in a grassy bowl at the lake. Fossil Mountain lies above to the west. Return as you ascended.

SIDEBAR: Fossil Ridge Wilderness Area

This 31,534 acre wilderness was designated by Congress in 1993 and named for a limestone ridge embedded with fossils that is above treeline.

Mill Lake.

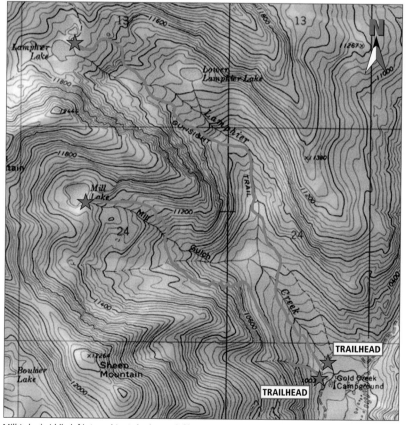

Mill Lake (middle left). Lamphier Lake (upper left).

95. Lamphier Lake

ROUND-TRIP DISTANCE	6 miles
HIKING TIME	Up in 85 minutes, down in 55 minutes
STARTING ELEVATION	10,030 feet
HIGHEST ELEVATION	11,710 feet
ELEVATION GAIN	1,820 feet (includes 70 extra feet each way)
DIFFICULTY	Moderate
MAPS	Trails Illustrated, Gunnison/Pitkin, Number 132 Fairview Peak 7.5 minute Gunnison County Number 5 Gunnison Basin Area – Gunnison National Forest

COMMENT: Lamphier Lake, in the Fossil Ridge Wilderness, is a high country jewel and the home of many fish. The major dividends of this hike are realized when you reach this magnificent lake, below several high peaks, after the trek up through the forest.

GETTING THERE: From U.S. 50, east of Gunnison, drive north from Parlin for 8.8 miles and turn left at the northern edge of Ohio City. Follow this road (Gunnison 771) for 7.0 miles into the Gold Creek campground. Cross Lamphier Creek and within 50 yards park on the left at a sign to Lamphier Lake.

THE HIKE: Begin to the north from the trail register and signboard. This is called the South Lottis Trail.

Follow the blocked, rocky road as it runs upward through the forest, with several crossings of Lamphier Creek. Aspen trees are abundant in the lower third of the hike.

Once you reach the upper basin, Lamphier Lake will appear down to your left. A faint, short trail leads to its banks. The main trail continues up and to the north, passing to the right of an unnamed pond above Lamphier Lake and on to another pass, called Gunsight. At the lake you may be lucky enough to see many good-sized fish swimming in the clear water. Fossil Mountain rises steeply to the south, Squaretop Mountain lies to the west, and Broncho Mountain north-northeast to the right of Gunsight Pass. Return as you ascended.

Lamphier Lake.

PHOTO BY BOB WATKINS

SEE MAP PAGE 203

96. Leon Lake

ROUND-TRIP DISTANCE	2.6 miles
HIKING TIME	Out in 25 minutes, back in 25 minutes
STARTING ELEVATION	10,490 feet
HIGHEST ELEVATION	10,550 feet
ELEVATION GAIN	390 feet (includes 330 extra feet)
DIFFICULTY	Easy
MAPS	Trails Illustrated, Grand Mesa, Number 136 Leon Peak 7.5 minute Mesa County Number 4 Grand Mesa National Forest

COMMENT: The Grand Mesa, with over 200 lakes, is a fantastic outdoor playground east of Grand Junction. This hike to Leon Lake is easy, scenic, and clearly marked. It provides an introduction to this often-overlooked paradise. Grand Mesa receives considerable rainfall and the area is often lush and moist. Bicycles and ATVs are forbidden on this trail.

GETTING THERE: On Colorado 65, between Interstate Highway 70 (exit 49), with Mesa on the north and Cedaredge on the south, drive to the main visitor center on Grand Mesa and turn east onto Forest Road 121. Follow Road 121 for 8.7 miles past several lovely lakes. Then turn right onto Road 126 and follow this road 2.8 miles to road end at the Leon Lake trailhead, within the Weir and Johnson Campground. Park on the right, adjacent to the Weir and Johnson Reservoir.

THE HIKE: Start on foot to the north and cross the dam of the Weir and Johnson Reservoir. The Sackett Reservoir lies below, on your left. At the end of the dam, take the right fork and follow Trail 707 along the Weir and Johnson Reservoir. After about 100 yards, follow the trail as it leaves the reservoir and rises into the trees. Cross a small creek and continue to ascend easterly. Avoid a side trail on the left. Reach the highest point on this trail and then gently descend to a green meadow with the Leon Park Reservoir visible on the far right edge of the meadow. Ascend the trail again into the forest and rise to a ridge. From here it is a gentle descent to Leon Lake, which can be seen through the trees below, to the northeast. The lake is quite large and is said to have an abundant fish population. Leon Peak is the formidable summit to the left (west) of the lake. Return as you came.

Leon Lake.

PHOTO BY MARIA SMITH

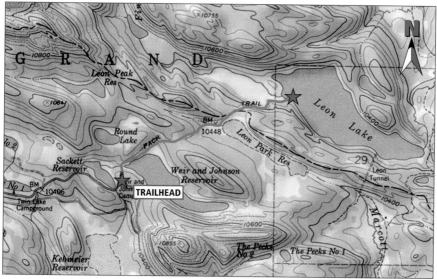

Leon Lake.

97. Navajo Lake

ROUND-TRIP DISTANCE	10.4 miles
HIKING TIME	Up in 165 minutes, down in 125 minutes
STARTING ELEVATION	9,325 feet
HIGHEST ELEVATION	11,360 feet
ELEVATION GAIN	3,295 feet (includes 1,260 extra feet)
DIFFICULTY	More difficult
MAPS	Trails Illustrated, Telluride/Silverton/Ouray/Lake City, Number 141 Dolores Peak 7.5 minute Dolores County Number 3 San Juan National Forest

COMMENT: The hike to Navajo Lake in the Lizard Head Wilderness is long, with considerable elevation gain. Your rewards include vast, lush meadows, abundant aspen, a lovely alpine lake, and soaring, high peaks. Navajo Lake is a popular camping site for mountain climbers. Three Fourteeners can be reached from Navajo Basin. These are Wilson Peak, Mount Wilson and El Diente Peak.

GETTING THERE: From Colorado 145, either drive south from Lizard Head Pass for 5.9 miles or north from Rico to the Dunton Road. Then turn northwest onto the Dunton Road (Road 535) and set your mileage to zero. Follow this narrow but well-graded road for a total of 7.2 miles. Then make a sharp right turn for another 0.1 mile and park at the Navajo Lake trailhead. En route to this trailhead, keep straight at mile 4.2 and pass some cabins on the right at mile 4.9 of the Dunton Road. (Road 535 continues southeast to Dolores and Colorado 145.)

THE HIKE: Start walking north past a trail register and soon pass the Groundhog Trail and a bridge on the left as you enter the Lizard Head Wilderness. After 0.75 mile, cross on a trio of logs the West Dolores River, flowing down from Navajo Lake. The trail then rises into a vast meadow with high grass, occasional groves of trees, and great vistas. Dolores Peak is the prominent, bald mountain on the left and unmistakable El Diente Peak ("The Tooth" in Spanish) is straight ahead. Your trail will lead to the left of the El Diente ridge. At mile 2.5, the Kilpacker Trail enters from the right, at the edge of the forest. Continue straight and the trail soon becomes steeper

Navajo Lake from above.

PHOTO BY DAVID HITE

as you rise to a fork and the highest elevation of this hike, at mile 4.6. The left fork ascends to Woods Lake; you begin your descent to Navajo Lake by the right fork. Pass some modest mine diggings on the left, shortly before reaching the scenic shore of Navajo Lake. With the El Diente – Mount Wilson ridge on the right, Gladstone Peak is the striking summit high above the basin to the east. The mountain on your left is unnamed thus far. The trail continues up into Navajo Basin to reach a pass at the Rock of Ages Mine. Enjoy the lake and restore your energy for the long return with some intermittent elevation gains.

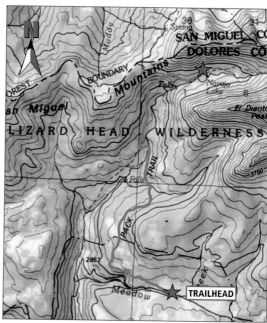

Navajo Lake.

98. Columbine Lake (LaPlata County)

ROUND-TRIP DISTANCE	6.2 miles up to Lower Chicago Basin, 2.9 more miles to Columbine Lake (9.1 miles each way)
HIKING TIME	230 minutes to Lower Chicago Basin, 105 minutes more to Columbine Lake, down to Lower Chicago Basin in 70 minutes, 165 minutes more down to Needleton.
STARTING ELEVATION	8,212 feet
HIGHEST ELEVATION	12,700 feet
ELEVATION GAIN	5,728 feet (includes 1,240 extra feet)
DIFFICULTY	Most difficult
MAPS	Trails Illustrated, Weminuche Wilderness, Number 140 Columbine Pass 7.5 minute Mountain View Crest 7.5 minute LaPlata County Number 3 San Juan National Forest

COMMENT: Every Colorado hiker should try to get up into Chicago Basin once in his or her lifetime. Although the trek is complicated and strenuous, the scenic rewards are great. After the train drops you off at Needleton, the hike, with an ample backpack, up the Needle Creek Trail into the Weminuche Wilderness, requires stamina. Once in Lower Chicago Basin, around 11,200 feet, you select a campsite with dazzling peaks, wild goats and flowing water all around you. The Needle Creek Trail then continues around to the right through numerous switchbacks and two vast meadows to lofty Columbine Pass and then down to Columbine Lake. The trail is exceptionally clear and well graded.

GETTING THERE: Take the Durango Silverton Narrow Gauge Train and get off at Needleton. (Call 970-247-2733 for information about this popular, historic tourist attraction.)

THE HIKE: Begin hiking across the bridge over the Animas River at Needleton and follow the wide Needle Creek Trail for 6.2 miles up into lovely Lower Chicago Basin, with Needle Creek always on your right. At Lower Chicago Basin, most parties will camp. To continue up to Columbine Pass, follow the main Needle Creek Trail and avoid the left fork, which ascends northwest up to Twin Lakes. This main trail curves right and crosses Needle Creek at the head of Lower Chicago Basin. Then ascend past mine tailings up into the trees. Pass an old mining tunnel and cabin and continue up through two

Columbine Lake from Columbine Pass.

PHOTO BY DAVID HITE

high, grassy meadows to a series of switchbacks leading to Columbine Pass. From here, descend left 350 feet on the Johnson Creek Trail to beautiful Columbine Lake. Enjoy all this wild beauty before retracing your route.

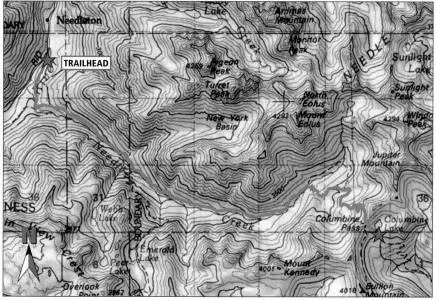

Columbine Lake.

99. The Blue Lakes

ROUND-TRIP DISTANCE	9.6 miles (Upper Lake)
HIKING TIME	Up in 160 minutes, down in 103 minutes
STARTING ELEVATION	9,400 feet
HIGHEST ELEVATION	11,710 feet
ELEVATION GAIN	2,960 feet (includes 325 extra feet each way)
DIFFICULTY	Moderate
MAPS	Trails Illustrated, Telluride/Silverton/Ouray/Lake City, Number 141 Telluride 7.5 minute Mount Sneffels 7.5 minute Ouray County Number 2 Uncompahgre National Forest

COMMENT: Whenever you are in the Ridgway, Ouray, or Telluride area, a beautiful lake and flowing water hike leads to the three Blue Lakes beneath towering Mount Sneffels in the wilderness area named after this Fourteener. The last half of July and the first half of August should be best times for flowers and rushing water.

GETTING THERE: From Colorado 62, between Ridgway on the north and Placerville on the south, drive south on the Dallas Creek Road (Ouray 7) for 8.8 miles to the Blue Lakes Trailhead. En route, keep left at mile 0.3 and at mile 1.6. Keep right at mile 2.0 and at mile 7.1. At mile 8.7, keep straight into the trailhead parking area. Regular cars can reach this trailhead.

THE HIKE: Begin on foot to the south and keep right at a signboard and register. The left fork is the Blaine Trail. Ascend the clear trail and pass a Mount Sneffels Wilderness sign after 1.3 miles. With many high peaks rimming the basin, continue up to Lower Blue Lake (10,950 feet) at mile 3.3. The bright blue color of the lake will impress you. A trail sign just before the lower lake directs you to the east and over East Dallas Creek, to the two higher lakes. The first part of this trail is rough and steep, before several switchbacks make the ascent easier. After passing timberline, you will pass Middle Blue Lake, (11,540 feet) below on the left before the final, gentle 0.3 mile rise to the Upper Blue Lake (11,690 feet). Mount Sneffels looms above to the north-northeast and the trail continues up to Blue Lakes Pass to the right of Mount Sneffels. Dallas Peak is impressive to the south. Enjoy this lovely high basin before returning as you ascended.

Lower Blue Lake from route to Middle Blue Lake.

PHOTO BY JOHN LACHER

The Blue Lakes.

213

100. Opal Lake

ROUND-TRIP DISTANCE	2.6 miles
HIKING TIME	Up in 35 minutes, down in 28 minutes
STARTING ELEVATION	8,731 feet
HIGHEST ELEVATION	9,260 feet
ELEVATION GAIN	769 feet (includes 240 extra feet)
DIFFICULTY	Easy
MAPS	Trails Illustrated, South San Juan/Del Norte, Number 142 Harris Lake 7.5 minute Archuleta County Number 3 San Juan National Forest

COMMENT: This easy hike lies in the San Juan Wilderness. Features include a lovely aspen grove and the unusual color of the lake. This green hue gives the lake its name and is due to the sediment from the Chalk Mountains that overlook and drain into the lake.

GETTING THERE: From U.S. 160 on the eastern edge of Pagosa Springs, drive south on U.S. 84 for 8 miles and turn left onto the Blanco Basin Road (Archuleta County Road 326). Set your odometer to zero. Follow this excellent dirt road up the valley and avoid side roads. Keep left at mile 8.5. Turn right at mile 9.7 from U.S. 84 and cross the Blanco River on a bridge. Continue straight at a four-way intersection and sign at mile 10.0. At mile 13, turn right at another sign and continue 0.7 mile further and park at the trailhead.

THE HIKE: The trail begins steeply to the east-northeast, past a signboard and a register. Stay on the main trail as it passes a wilderness sign in heavy forest. Make two creek crossings before entering a vast grove of tall aspens. Pass through an open meadow and avoid the narrow trail on your left. This path leads to Fish Creek. Cross White Creek again and quickly pass some beaver ponds on the left before rising to a modest high point, from which you can see Opal Lake. A quick and easy descent brings you to the lake. The trail continues past the right side of Opal Lake. Enjoy your lakeside respite before the easy return.

Opal Lake.

PHOTO BY ROSALYN SAMPLE

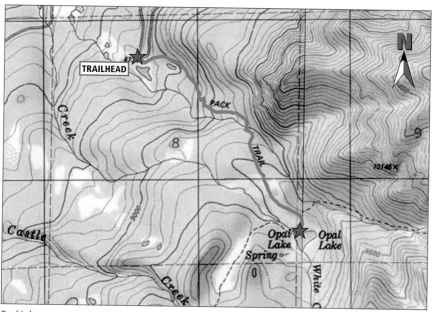

Opal Lake.

REFERENCES

Apt, Alan. *Afoot & Afield Denver/Boulder and Colorado's Front Range.* Oakland, CA: Wilderness Press, 2008.

Boddie, Caryn and Boddie, Peter. *Hiking Colorado.* Helena, Montana: Falcon Publishing Company, 1991.

Boddie, Caryn and Boddie, Peter. *Hiking Colorado II.* Helena, Montana: Falcon Publishing Company, 1999.

Brown, Robert L. *Uphill Both Ways.* Caldwell, Idaho: The Caxton Printers, Ltd., 1978.

Cushman, Ruth Carol and Cushman, Glenn. *Boulder Hiking Trails.* Boulder, Colorado: Pruett Publishing Company, 1995.

Dannen, Kent and Dannen, Donna. *Hiking Rocky Mountain National Park: Including Indian Peaks.* Old Saybrook, Connecticut: The Globe Pequot Press, 1994.

Davis, Lora. *Hiking Trails in the Collegiate Peaks Wilderness Area.* Boulder, Colorado: Pruett Publishing Company, 1994.

Fielder, John and Pearson, Mark. *The Complete Guide To Colorado's Wilderness Areas.* Englewood, Colorado: Westcliffe Publishers, Inc., 1995.

Foster, Lisa. *Rocky Mountain National Park: The Complete Hiking Guide.* Englewood, Colorado: Westcliffe Publishers, 2005.

Gilliland, Mary Ellen. *The Summit Hiker.* Silverthorne, Colorado: Alpenrose Press, 1997.

Gilliland, Mary Ellen. *The Vail Hiker.* Silverthorne, Colorado: Alpenrose Press, 1996.

Hagen, Mary. *Hiking Trails of Northern Colorado.* Boulder, Colorado: Pruett Publishing Company, 1987.

Heasley, John E. *Colorado's Indian Peaks Wilderness.* Fort Collins, Colorado: RAS Publishing, 1999.

Jones, Tom Lorang. *Colorado's Continental Divide Trail.* Englewood, Colorado: Westcliffe Publishers, Inc., 1997.

Lowe, Don and Lowe Roberta. *50 West Central Colorado Hiking Trails.* Beaverton, Oregon: The Touchstone Press, 1976.

Lowe, Don and Lowe, Roberta. *80 Northern Colorado Hiking Trails.* Beaverton, Oregon: The Touchstone Press, 1973.

Malitz, Jerome. *Rocky Mountain National Park Dayhikers Guide.* Boulder, Colorado: Johnson Books, 1993.

Marlowe, Al. *A Hiking and Camping Guide to the Flat Tops Wilderness.* Boulder, Colorado: Fred Pruett Books, 1994.

Martin, Bob. *Hiking Trails of Central Colorado.* Boulder, Colorado: Pruett Publishing Company, 1983.

Molvar, Erik. *Hiking Colorado's Maroon Bells-Snowmass Wilderness.* Guilford, Connecticut: Globe Pequot Press, 2001.

Ohlrich, Warren. *Aspen and Central Colorado Trails.* Basalt, Colorado: WHO Press, 1999.

Pixler, Paul. *Hiking Trails of Southwestern Colorado.* Boulder, Colorado: Pruett Publishing Company, 1981.

Tarr, M. A. *Timber, Talus and Tundra.* Gunnison, Colorado: Uncompahgre Books, 1996.

Thompson, Jay and Thompson, Therese. *Hiker's Guide to the Mount Zirkel Wilderness.* Boulder, Colorado: Pruett Publishing Company, 1992.

Warren, Scott S. *100 Hikes in Colorado.* Seattle, Washington: the Mountaineers, 1995.

ABOUT THE AUTHOR

 DAVE MULLER is a Denver psychiatrist who has written *Colorado Summit Hikes for Everyone, The Colorado Year Round Outdoor Guide,* and *Colorado's Quiet Winter Trails.* From 1988 until 2005 he wrote the weekly Hike, Cross-Country, or Showshoe Tour of the Week for *The Denver Post.* From Washington D.C. via Texas, he rejoices his move to Colorado over 39 years ago.

INDEX